To my dear friend
Dan,
Who makes the
Puntillo Christmas true
look amazing year after year
Thank you for your
generosity of time and talent
We appreciate you so

Love Maddie & A

Italy
on a
Plate

Travels, Memories, Menus

SUSAN GRAVELY

VIETRI Founder

VIETRI

PUBLISHING

Edited by Brette Baumhover, Lisa Boyles,
Holli Draughn, Heather Hutchins, and Janice Shay

Book and cover design by Mollie Baker

Lifestyle photography by Infraordinario Photo
Food photography by Food Seen

Publication consultant: Janice Shay

Library of Congress Control Number: 2022914167

ISBN: 978-1-7321133-6-7
First Edition
Printed in Canada by Friesens Corporation

VIETRI Publishing
343 Elizabeth Brady Road
Hillsborough, NC 27278

VIETRI.com

DEDICATION

I dedicate this book to my parents and my siblings. Lee and Lee, my mother and father, were loving and strict, worldly and down-to-earth. Frances, Steve, and Page, my sister and two brothers, were caring and fun-loving. Our family mealtimes were spent together, around a table, discussing ideas. It was there that we learned about a bigger world, that we had a place in it, and that Southern hospitality and good manners were important. There would be no *Italy on a Plate* without them.

TABLE *of* CONTENTS

FOREWORD
by Frances Mayes

WHEN SUSAN ARRIVES IN ITALY, SHE IS NOT OUT of the airport before she starts fielding calls. Everyone wants to see La Susanna. Business, yes, but it only begins there. In her many years of traveling to Italy, sometimes two or three times a year for long visits, she has made friends up and down the peninsula. Great friends. What a privilege to have the opportunity to share their pasta in the kitchen in Umbria, attend lavish feasts at long tables in a vineyard in Tuscany, grab coffee with artists in Rome, spread picnics on the Amalfi beaches, hit all the amazing restaurants in Friuli-Venezia Giulia, and sip a spritz on a balcony in Venice. All with her people.

Susan came to Italy originally on vacation with her mother and sister Frances. On that fateful trip, they discovered by chance the charming ceramics of the south of Italy. Soon, they started VIETRI on a whim. A very smart whim that inspired a passion.

The decision—impossible to know these things from the start—resulted in the great business that is VIETRI. The "Gravely girls" knew that artisan ceramic tradition goes to the very roots of Italian culture. In museums all over the country, you see the aesthetic designs practiced by the early Etruscans and by the invading Greeks who settled along the Ionian Sea. Their earthenware pots and plates, cups and bowls all show that it was beauty that motivated the making of everyday objects. You want to reach inside the glass cases and touch that sculptural pitcher, that handsome water jug. By the mid-14th century, glazing and decorating had begun. During the Renaissance, ceramic design flourished, and many of the complex patterns established then endure today.

Opposite page: Author Susan Gravely with friend and author Frances Mayes outside her Tuscan villa, Bramasole.

Now, there is a new culture of design, still aimed toward enhancing daily life. Susan's passionate quest remains: What will delight, what will be the best gift, what adds to the creative tradition? The versatile and imaginative dinnerware she and her team commission or discover lifts the spirits and ensures that gathering at a table will be not just dinner, but an occasion. Why did I once think I would have an everyday set of dishes and a formal set? Living in Italy, and inspired, too, by VIETRI, I came to realize that I loved variety on my table. After all, you don't just have two pairs of shoes—one pair of trainers and one fancier! Every day the table is set. A colorful collection of patterns, linens, and glassware just enlivens the dinner and keeps you enjoying where you pull up your chair to eat with those you love. My own adoration of ceramics resulted in a kitchen expansion!

Frances has now retired but still travels frequently to Italy, especially to Florence. Now, Susan constantly comes for her work, but work and play are seamless. I get the impression that, regardless of projects, she would be tearing up and down from Puglia to Valle d'Aosta. She has a gift for locating artisan designers of ceramics, sure, but an equal gift for making friends. Her secret talent? She is genuinely interested in the other person. Immediately, she wants to know who you really are, your interests, your family, your dreams and ideas, where you are headed and where you have been. There is no slow wading into a friendship; Susan goes in off the high dive. As E. M. Forster advised, "Only connect," though Susan hardly needs his wisdom. This book— part memoir, part travel lore, part introduction to friends—is a loving tribute to the good life we find around a table.

Our feasts are our memories. We gather around to only connect and to celebrate. *Italy on a Plate*—well, yes! This book is a joyous testament to Susan's warm, fun, adventurous personality and reveals to us just how close to the heart her friends are. I am lucky to be among them.

Opposite page: The cypress tree-lined path leading up to Xenia Lemos's agriturismo, Casetta, in the hills of Tuscany.

INTRODUCTION

I GREW UP IN A HOME FILLED WITH GUESTS, dinner parties, and Southern hospitality. My parents coincidentally shared "Lee" as their first name, so they were known around our hometown of Rocky Mount, North Carolina, as She Lee and He Lee. To me, they were Momma and Daddy, and they were the best parents in the world to my sister, Frances, to my brothers, Steve and Page, and to me.

Momma was a gracious and graceful hostess. She loved welcoming my father's business partners from around the world into our home. My father worked in the tobacco trade, so these visitors came to us from Egypt, Thailand, Norway, Saudi Arabia, Zimbabwe, and beyond. Many of my earliest memories are of Frances and me helping to set a beautiful table for guests, with everything from tablecloths, silverware, and heirloom dinnerware to flower arrangements collected from the garden. The menu was also carefully planned. I remember perfectly cooked filet mignon, baked potatoes with butter, fresh mushrooms in red wine sauce, asparagus, homemade rolls, and—depending on the season—lemon chess pie, hot milk cake with chocolate icing, or pecan pie for dessert. Momma's instruction and attention to preparation and presentation taught us the value in making others feel warmly welcomed at our table.

Frances and I were allowed to join these dinner parties if we behaved ourselves. How we loved listening to guests' stories of life from other parts of the world. The visitors often

became part of our family, and I remember them attending our sporting events and giving speeches at our schools about their own countries. After the visitors returned home, my father would pull out a globe to show us from where they had come. As he pointed out these distant countries, he would always say, "The world is really small; no matter where you are, you're only a plane ride or phone call away." He wanted us to feel interested in the world and excited to explore its many treasures.

That curiosity and enthusiasm for adventure certainly lived in my parents. They were avid travelers and visited many countries in their 35 years of marriage. They loved the sights of Venice, Florence, and Rome, of Cairo, Dubrovnik, and the French countryside. Unfortunately, their time together was cut short by my father's early death at age 60 from a heart attack. My family grieved together, and after two years, my mother decided on a fitting tribute to the memory of her beloved husband and our wonderful father: We would go on the trip she had always wanted to take with him. My mother had her sights set on a hotel on the Amalfi Coast that she had read about in *Bon Appétit* magazine—Il San Pietro di Positano, designed and owned by Carlo Cinque—and she added Rome, Florence, and Venice to the itinerary. In May of 1983, Momma, Frances, and I set off for Italy with no idea that this trip

The Gravely family at home, 1954. Opposite page: Steve, Lee, Frances, Susan, and Lee Gravely at home in Rocky Mount, NC, 1957; Lee and Lee Gravely in Venice's Saint Mark's Square, 1960.

would completely transform the rest of our lives. Our brothers were jealous for sure!

Our adventure started on the airplane. The three of us took our seats together in coach, and we busied ourselves with schedules and plans for the weeks ahead. Frances, the daring and sparkling counter to my more serious, rule-abiding self, needed the restroom, and she sashayed her way up the aisle to business class with her usual glamour and style. When she was ready to return, a beverage cart blocked the path to her seat, and as she waited, she struck up a conversation with an Italian gentleman sitting by the aisle next to where she stood. Frances told him of our family's plans, and he asked questions about what we hoped to see and do. The gentleman seemed charmed by Frances's zest and excitement. When she returned to her seat, my sister enjoyed telling us about the interesting encounter.

About an hour later, we were chatting away when that same gentleman appeared by our seats and introduced himself as Fabio Puccinelli. He offered us some restaurant recommendations in Rome, the first stop on our trip, and he gave Momma his business card. He told us it would be his honor to take us to dinner when we made it to his town of Florence, and Momma, with no intention of ever taking him up on it, warmly thanked him and tucked the card away in her pocketbook. After a bit more conversation, he returned to his seat, and we continued our journey, never dreaming we would see him again—though we would certainly try his suggested restaurants!

After a delightful and fascinating few days

in Rome, the next stop on our journey was Positano on the Amalfi Coast. I remember being driven through the hills from Naples to Positano with Momma and Frances, and as we approached the small winding road overlooking the Tyrrhenian Sea, we caught a breathtaking glimpse of the village through the trees. We saw pastel houses perched on cliffs descending into the sparkling cerulean sea. We all agreed we must have died and gone to heaven because we had never seen anything so beautiful. Thus began our infatuation with the famed Amalfi Coast and Positano in particular.

When we arrived at the flat top of a cliff by a sign for Il San Pietro, several white-coated men greeted us with, "Buongiorno, Signore Gravely!" and escorted us along moss-edged steps to a small, discreet elevator. The elevator took us down through the rocks of the cliff to the entrance of the hotel. Despite our high hopes and long-held

Steve, Frances, Page, and Susan at Thanksgiving, 1966.
Opposite page: Frances, Susan, and Lee on their first trip to Positano, 1983.

expectations, we were not prepared for the beauty before us: deep pink bougainvillea hanging from a white plaster ceiling, dark stone floors, antique tables, white cotton-covered furniture, brightly painted local art, and a flower-filled garden overlooking the sea.

Our rooms had windows with views of the ocean, bathrooms drenched in colorful tile, and the elegance of soft white and aqua fabrics everywhere. Momma stayed in the hotel's most prized room, number 23, which had belonged to Carlo Cinque. It featured wraparound windows that displayed the majesty of the Tyrrhenian Sea and the Positano

beach. The only thing that would have made the room better would have been having my father there to enjoy it with her. One of my favorite pictures that sits on my bookshelf to this day is of Frances and Momma sitting together in a swing on that room's terrace.

The visual feast continued that evening at dinner. The hotel's dining room was aglow with light reflecting off the sea, and the tables were covered in peach-colored tablecloths with crisp white napkins and a few sprigs of draping bougainvillea in vases. What especially took our eye, however, was the array of colorful plates on

The view of the Amalfi Coast from the terrace of Il San Pietro di Positano;
Campagna, VIETRI's flagship dinnerware collection.
Opposite page: Frances and Lee on the terrace at Il San Pietro di Positano, 1983.

each table. The plates shared a gentle, ruffled edge and a similar palette of cheerful, Mediterranean hues, each adorned with a different design— flowers, animals, fruits, and more. We had never seen tableware so beautiful.

For us, this was it! As a family who enjoyed entertaining with grace, good food, and a gorgeous table, this experience was both familiar and the pinnacle of hospitality. Dinner began with an oven-fired pizza, and it continued with fresh sea bass, small potatoes, and perfectly prepared seasonal vegetables. The service was warm and generous, the ambiance sparkled like the sea below us, but—more than anything—it was the plates! Even writing this, my heart beats a bit faster remembering the excitement of that night, which so reflected what our parents had taught us: that the world is indeed full of wonders to discover and celebrate.

The three of us were so taken by the dinnerware that we asked our waiter about its origin. He explained that each plate was handpainted by local artisans in the nearby town of Vietri sul Mare, and, picking up on our enthusiasm, he asked if we would be interested in visiting the factory. Would we ever! We immediately made plans to hire a bilingual driver and visit the following day. We spent our first full day on the Amalfi Coast in an amazing factory, watching men and women of all ages create magic with their hands and paintbrushes. We were dazzled and delighted.

During our remaining time in glorious Positano, we wandered the cobblestone streets, dined at the beachfront restaurants, shopped for gifts, and marveled at this village of many colors, creations, and craftsmanship. Even with all the extravagant beauty we encountered, we kept coming back to the area's vibrant and whimsical handpainted dinnerware, and we wondered how we could enjoy its magic in our daily lives. There was nothing like it in America at the time, and we knew everyone back home would love it as much as we did. How could we share it? Could we take individual orders for specific people? Should we open a retail store? A wholesale business? We knew we had come across something special, and our minds and conversations were humming with various possibilities. As the ideas percolated, we decided we would fill a large trunk with as much dinnerware as possible so that we could mull over the options with the beautiful plates in hand back at home. Frances and I spent one and a half more days at the factory selecting sample pieces to fill a trunk—four animal designs to intermix on a table plus a floral design. If we could have sent back some of the incredible Italian food, we would have done that, too!

Another moment of serendipity in Positano came when Momma, Frances, and I were having a cocktail in the Il San Pietro's beautiful sitting room. An older couple came into the room, and we began to chat with them. They were Aileen and George Karp, and we learned they were from New York City. Mr. Karp ran a high-end clothing wholesale company, and Frances and I began to pepper him with questions about running a business. We shared our idea of importing plates like those used in the hotel, and Mr. Karp listened intently. After asking Frances and me about our

Susan and Lee with former VIETRI Agent Ferdinando Mannetti and Don Vincenzo Solimene of the Solimene factory, 1990; Toni Solimene and Susan negotiating, 1995. Opposite page: Silvio Solimene, Susan, and Frances admiring maestro Giuseppe Potenza's painting at the Solimene factory, 1986.

vision and goals, he told us he thought a wholesale business would be perfect for us. He also gave us the gift of confidence; he told us he knew we would be very successful due to the palpable excitement and enthusiasm we had for the products. To this day, I credit Mr. Karp for giving us the big push to turn our vacation dream into something real.

Eventually, it was time to leave our now-beloved Positano, and we headed to Florence. We took to the streets immediately, soaking in the sights and shopping for paper products, leather goods, clothes, and more. We had meals that were out-of-this-world delicious, and after our dinner at the famed Ristorante Buca Lapi, we decided to walk home, arm-in-arm, to our hotel just three blocks away. Momma was walking on the outside, closest to the street, and suddenly we heard a scooter zooming up behind us. Before we knew what had happened, the rider grabbed Momma's pocketbook off her arm and whizzed away into the night. Fortunately, Momma was unharmed, but we realized with great dismay that not only was the pocketbook now gone, but also our passports and all our traveler's checks. Younger readers might not know, but losing one's traveler's checks is the modern equivalent of losing your phone, credit cards, checks, and cash. This was not a good situation.

We rushed back to the hotel, and the concierge put us in a taxi headed to the police station. Once there, it seemed the policemen were more interested in flirting with Frances and me than

chasing down the mystery rider who was probably far, far away by now. We returned to the hotel deflated and beyond discouraged. With two days before our departure for Venice, we were in trouble. Sitting in the hotel lobby, we discussed our plight and possible solutions. We needed some inside assistance, but we knew no one in Florence.

Except... We all stopped—that man we had met on the plane! Maybe he would help us?

Thankfully, Momma had transferred his card from her pocketbook to her suitcase earlier in the trip. She retrieved the card, and we called his number. No answer. We had a glass of wine to calm our frazzled nerves and waited. We called again. No answer. It was getting late, but we decided to keep trying, as we didn't have any other options. Finally, Fabio Puccinelli answered the telephone, and Momma told him our situation. Despite the late hour, he immediately offered to help us and arrived soon thereafter in our hotel lobby. After hearing the story again, he calmly promised to arrange for us to get new passports and new traveler's checks the next morning. Apparently, he was a well-connected man in Florence, so we were cautiously hopeful and extremely grateful for his help. Over the next two days, he miraculously helped us procure new passports and traveler's checks. This would be the first, but not the last, time that Fabio navigated the Italian way for us. Thanks to him, we were able to continue our trip with a final stop in Venice, where we reveled in the architecture, history, and extraordinary food of that magical city.

Eventually, our fairy-tale trip concluded and

we returned home to North Carolina. We excitedly unpacked the dinnerware we had brought home from Positano and eagerly showed it to our friends. They immediately expressed interest in owning these unique and colorful handpainted pieces, so it was then and there, in 1983, that Momma, Frances, and I decided to import the dinnerware to sell to retail stores across the US. The wholesale business was somewhat familiar to us, as that was what my father had done in the tobacco industry, so the trip truly came full circle in our mission of honoring his love and legacy.

My mother, Frances, and I decided to name the company VIETRI, a tribute to the town where it all began and a play on the phrase *Tre Vite*, which is Italian for "three lives." Then, the hard work began. We knew we needed an Italian on our team, and we were beyond thrilled when our one Italian friend and Florentine rescuer, Fabio Puccinelli, took a chance on us and our idea and agreed to become our agent in September 1983.

Frances and I soon returned to Vietri sul Mare to negotiate the logistical details of ordering dinnerware, and while we hardly understood a word of the discussions, we trusted Fabio to guide us. It didn't take an interpreter, however, to realize that we had come to an impasse with the factory on pricing. They thought our offers were too low, and we thought their prices too high. The days of our trip were ticking by, and we could not find a number upon which to agree. After days of this stalemate, Fabio loaded Frances and me up in the car to drive to a nearby town to get a calculator. It was such an old relic that it had to be cranked by hand! Even so, we were grateful for it, and we spent two days literally cranking the numbers to

determine the range of prices we needed to start VIETRI. On the very last morning of our trip, we returned to the factory with our prices in hand and Frances's best negotiating skills ready. Hallelujah, they accepted! We signed and officially had our first container of dinnerware ordered. We named it Campagna, Italian for countryside, in honor of the beauty of Italy's landscapes.

We returned home and spent the next few months learning everything we could about the wholesale business from anyone who would lend an ear. We filled notebooks with everything from customs broker information to names of shipping lines to how a profit and loss statement works. And then it was time to sell.

I had my sights set on the October New York Tabletop Show at the Prince George Hotel. It was notoriously difficult to secure a booth there, especially as a new, unproved business. I discovered the name of the gentleman in charge of running the show, Mr. Gene Wolfe, and I immediately called him to see if VIETRI could have a small space. He told me there was a long waiting list and it would be impossible to get a booth this late in the game. I persisted and told him I could be in New York the next day; could I please come show him what I was selling? With reluctance, he told me yes, so I quickly booked a flight and brought my 12 beautiful sample plates into the city.

We met the following morning, and I gave

him my best pitch. Fortunately, he decided to give us a chance. The only remaining space in the venue was a tiny nook right beside the registration table. We could have it under one condition: We had to make the space look great. We were in—VIETRI was going to be at the New York Tabletop Show!

Momma came to help me set up our postage stamp-size space, and we called upon our most stylish New York friends to let us borrow a table, hutch, and throw rug for our booth to make the space feel like a lovely home. I then came across a waiter at the Prince George who looked Italian. Indeed he was, so I hired him to come by the booth and charm customers with his Italian accent and pours of Chianti.

I think Daddy or some kind angel was smiling down on us, because who first happened upon our tiny booth but the elegantly dressed, very sophisticated buyers for Neiman Marcus. They were enchanted by the artful and cheerful handpainted designs and placed an order for $12,000 worth of dinnerware right there on the spot. It was $12 million dollars as far as we were concerned! We were gobsmacked, grateful, and in business.

With the promise of a successful venture, I realized that I had to learn Italian. I knew nothing about the language, but I did know that the University of North Carolina at Chapel Hill had a language department. I looked up the office in the phone book and ended up speaking with a gentleman who taught Italian at the university—and yes, he said, in fact he was taking a group of students to Taormina in Sicily to study. Taormina? Sicily? I had no idea where that was, but I signed up and set off to join a group of rowdy undergraduates who had no intention of going to class or studying. Day after day, I got up, went to class, and was taught alone (the college students elected other pastimes). I felt sorry for the professor—I am sure he wondered where the "real" students were—but I was glad to be there and to establish the foundation for my Italian.

We returned home and spent the next few months learning everything we could about the wholesale business from anyone who would lend an ear.

To make the most of my time in that part of the world, Fabio decided to come to Taormina and meet me every afternoon after class. We would hop in his dilapidated, non-air-conditioned car and drive from dusty village to dusty village looking for ceramic factories—and we found many! We had a fantastic time discovering local artisans, trying the local cuisines, and marveling at Italian creativity.

After I returned home, our first container with everything we had ordered the

previous spring arrived from Italy. It was March 12, 1984, and I will never forget that day. Momma, then 58, brought her close friends from Rocky Mount to help us unpack the container. Frances and I asked our friends and some college students to lend a hand. We still needed more workers, so I drove to a bus stop nearby and beckoned folks standing around to come join the effort for eight dollars an hour.

We created an inventory list and tried to organize the products as carefully as we could. We opened hundreds and hundreds of boxes and tallied every item in a paper notebook. After we had counted each piece, we thanked our unique staff and let them get back to the rest of their day.

Momma, Frances, and I stayed to pick the large Neiman Marcus order. We had started VIETRI, and we were beyond thrilled. Neiman Marcus, our very first customer, continues to be a VIETRI customer to this day.

The company that began with just Frances, Momma, and me has grown to more than 75 employees and is now America's largest Italian ceramics importer. Our family's story has been described as a modern day fairy-tale, and our products can be found in more than 2,000 specialty retailers and department stores in all 50 states and internationally. We have been featured in top magazines such as *House Beautiful, Oprah, Elle Decor, Brides,* and *Coastal Living,* and we have been inducted into the ARTS Award Hall of Fame for our creative designs.

Since those earliest adventures, I have traveled throughout Italy from the southernmost tip of Sicily to the northernmost towns of the Lombardy region and have become fluent in Italian. Collectively, I've been lucky enough to spend years in this favorite country of mine, and Italy's spirit continues to enchant me. Its enthusiasm, passion, style, and romance live in its people, and, through my work, I have met many incredible Italians and enjoyed so many delicious home-cooked meals. These people have become as dear to me as family. I have attended their weddings, children's birthdays, and Sunday evening family dinners around their kitchen tables. To be invited into people's homes, to share a meal, to celebrate life's big and small moments together... these memories are some of the most cherished in

my life. These connections have been the happiest and most unexpected result of creating VIETRI, and for them I am profoundly grateful.

In 2023, VIETRI celebrates 40 years of business. In honor of four incredible decades, and with gratitude for my Italian friends who have welcomed me into their lives, their homes, and to their tables for good food, fine wine, and cherished companionship, I have written this memoir and cookbook. Thanks to their kindness, hospitality, and generosity, my friends have shared the recipes found in this book. I hope these wonderful dishes and the personal stories of our time together will bring you the same comfort, warmth, and joy they have brought me.

Frances and Susan, 2017.
Opposite page: Susan and Lee
in Rome, 1984.

CHAPTER 1

A Love Affair in Florence
TITA BOSIO, TUSCANY

WISE AND WARM, SENSIBLE AND SINCERE, CREATIVE AND
curious, Tita Bosio is someone I deeply admire and am so grateful to have met in
my Italian travels. It's perfectly fitting that our paths crossed on my first trip to
Italy because I truly cannot imagine the past 40 years of my life—or VIETRI as a
company—without her influence, insight, and inspiration. An established member
of Florentine society, Tita is both respectful of old-world Florence and also an
innovative thinker, serial entrepreneur, and champion of new nonprofit initiatives.

My friendship with Tita began in 1983 in the hills of Florence around 11 o'clock
in the evening. Frances and I had been at dinner with our new friend and soon-to-
be agent, Fabio, and we were discussing our ceramic business dreams. Fabio, as if
struck by lightning, leapt up and said that he must take us to meet his dear friend
Tita immediately, as she was a home décor buyer for Macy's and would certainly
have good advice for us. We couldn't wait to meet her, never mind the fact that it
was approaching midnight! We drove up a curving road high above the city until
we found a tree-lined pathway with an elegant wrought iron gate at the end. We
entered, and Fabio parked the car in front of a beautiful, traditional Italian villa.
Frances and I learned that Tita had inherited the top floor of the villa at the age of
18 and was now raising her three young children there.

We climbed the four flights of stairs to Tita's front door and knocked. Despite
the late hour, she graciously opened the door, invited us in, and listened to us two

*Tita and Susan inside
Tita's home.
Opposite page: Tita's Villa
in Florence.*

American girls talk giddily about our hopes and plans to sell the dinnerware we had found in Positano back in the US. She was very familiar with the pieces that had so delighted us, and while she never discouraged us, she gave us her honest opinion that it would be a challenge to work with these small Italian factories that were used to small, local orders. She was not wrong, and I think of her word of caution near daily as we try to negotiate our Italian orders, timetables, and deliveries!

We talked into the wee hours that night, and both Frances and I knew that we had met someone truly special. Since that initial meeting, Tita has been my sounding board, source of comfort, and fellow adventurer. Despite being part of traditional Florentine society, she has always looked for new opportunities and embodies a perspective of "why not try it?" rather than an attitude of complacency. I've seen her enthusiasm and open-mindedness time and time again as she launches new businesses, raises awareness and funds for mental health philanthropies in Italy, and has taken up boxing lessons in her 80s to stay fit and agile.

Many years ago, Tita and her sister Sofia co-owned a tiny jewelry store,

Scenes from inside Tita's home, including a portrait of her as a young equestrian.

Tita's dining room.
Opposite page: Inside Tita's home.

Lo Spillo, right off Florence's Ponte Vecchio. A literal jewel box, the sisters filled the three-square-meter space with unique and gorgeous pieces of jewelry. The store was so small that only one customer could fit in at a time!

I loved to visit her there, and I came to her in 1985 with a mission. I had just been in Milan, and while shopping there, I happened upon a fabulous necklace. I had never seen anything like it. It featured a collection of loose pearls enclosed in a tube of black mesh. I presented it to her with great excitement and asked if she would be able to create something similar in large quantities so that VIETRI could sell them. Most of the time, I am focused on finding and designing the most beautiful Italian home and garden products for VIETRI. However, sometimes I fall so deeply in love with an Italian product in a completely different category that I can't resist adding it to our catalog! That was the case with this unique necklace. I knew our customers would fall for it as I had. Tita had many pearls and beads she could use, but the mesh netting seemed hard to source. Not to be deterred, Tita scoured markets and stores for the right kind of material, and she eventually found what she was looking for in an automobile repair shop, of all places. The car shop used mesh tubing for some of their repairs, and the repairmen were happy to sell some to her.

Tita then began making the necklaces in different sizes and styles. We called it the Perla necklace, and, as I expected, it sold extremely well. I still adore and wear mine often. One time, I was wearing mine on a flight when a man flagged me down. He admired my necklace and said he wanted to buy one for his wife. Only a little later in conversation did I learn that he was a Supreme Court Justice! Upon my return home, I promptly sent him one to give to his wife. Since then, and even still today, I am stopped often by people who admire this simple but beautiful necklace. Though the beloved piece was discontinued many years ago, we are excited to start offering it to our customers again soon. They are being made by Tita's daughter-in-law. A family tradition!

I also had the privilege of being involved in another one of Tita's business ventures. Tita and her sisters inherited their grandmother's old Italian home and all its incredible furniture, antiques, art, and more. With her sisters' blessings, Tita decided to open a stand and start selling her grandmother's pieces at Florence's famed Piazza dei Ciompi, the oldest flea market in Florence. She ran a successful business at the market, and I had the great pleasure of traveling around Italy with her to source new treasures to sell over the years. I remember trips to Bologna where we discovered beautiful, unusual antiques with great history to bring back to Florence. Tita has an incredible eye for quality and artistry, and the triumph of her antiques stand is testament to her hard work and vision.

In soft shades of green, orange, and terra cotta, the painted wood floors bring great interest to the room, and the best part is that Tita did them herself!

As if these business ventures didn't keep Tita busy enough, she also found time to dedicate huge efforts toward philanthropy. She was responsible for opening Florence's Progetto Itaca, the city's first nonprofit dedicated to supporting those affected by mental health issues. Tita has used her long-standing connections in the region to raise funds and awareness for the cause, and I know that Italy is much the better for it.

While she does have fine taste and a deep Florentine network, one of Tita's most admirable qualities is her lack of pretension. She greets guests with an open door and without fussy formality. She exudes genuine ease with her friends and family, and I cannot count the number of times she's invited me over for lunch or dinner with an unselfconscious and warm, "Susan, come over! I've only made a soup, but come, come over!"

We often eat in her sun-filled, inviting kitchen. One particularly delightful design detail in the room is the stenciled floor. In soft shades of green, orange, and terra cotta, the painted wood floors bring great interest to the room, and the best part is that Tita did them herself! I remember when she was in the middle of the project, on hands and knees, carefully tracing each little shape. The kitchen's walls are a soft green, and they serve as a perfect complement to the tops of the trees that one sees looking out of the room's open windows. On the table, Tita favors a soft linen tablecloth with a vase of fresh flowers at the center. The room is like Tita—friendly, approachable, comforting. These qualities are mirrored in the food she serves as well. Like all Italians, Tita's recipes showcase the bounty of the current season and

Opposite page: The plans for Tita's hand-stenciled floors and the final product.

rely on nature's flavors to be the stars on the plate. She has been making many of her favorite recipes for more than 50 years, and she has perfected them down to each detail.

I hope Tita's inquisitive, interested attitude will encourage you to try something new and make some of her favorite recipes to offer your own family and friends a taste of Florence.

INSALATA DI KIWI
Kiwi Salad

Harvested beginning in late October, kiwis are a favorite seasonal fruit in Italy. They brighten this salad and complement the sweet and nutty taste of the Swiss cheese.

Serves 8

Preheat the oven to 350 degrees F.

Place the bacon on a greased, rimmed baking sheet and bake for 15 minutes until crispy. Drain on a paper towel-lined plate. Once cool, dice the bacon and set aside.

To prepare the salad, layer the spinach, cheese, kiwis, and pine nuts in a large salad bowl.

Whisk together the olive oil, salt, pepper, and lemon juice in a small bowl until fully combined.

When ready to serve, sprinkle the salad with the bacon and gently toss with the dressing. Let the salad sit for 10 minutes before serving.

INGREDIENTS

6 slices bacon

10 ounces fresh spinach,
washed and patted dry

1½ cups diced
Swiss or Emmental cheese

3 kiwis,
peeled and thinly sliced

1 tablespoon pine nuts

½ cup extra virgin
olive oil

½ teaspoon salt

Freshly ground black
pepper to taste

1 tablespoon
fresh lemon juice

ZUCCHINE AL GORGONZOLA
Zucchini with Gorgonzola

Zucchini pairs beautifully with many of Italy's regional cheeses. In the Veneto region, Asiago cheese is a delicious choice instead of Gorgonzola. In Tuscany, Pecorino is often used.

Serves 8

Preheat the oven to 375 degrees F.

Heat the oil in a large skillet to 325 degrees F over medium-high heat. Lightly fry the zucchini, a few at a time. Drain the fried zucchini on a paper towel-lined platter.

Arrange the zucchini in a lightly greased 8 x 8-inch baking dish. Season with salt and pepper.

In a small mixing bowl, mash Gorgonzola with a fork. Add the parsley, eggs, sour cream, and Parmigiano-Reggiano cheese. Stir to fully combine and pour over the zucchini.

Bake for 20 to 25 minutes, until the top begins to brown, and serve warm.

INGREDIENTS

2 cups extra virgin olive oil

2 pounds small zucchini, cut into ¼ inch thick rounds

Butter, for greasing dish

1 teaspoon salt

½ teaspoon black pepper

1¼ cups Gorgonzola

2 teaspoons finely chopped Italian parsley

2 large eggs

¾ cup sour cream

2 tablespoons grated Parmigiano-Reggiano cheese

STRUDEL DI CAROTE E ZUCCHINE
Carrot and Zucchini Strudel

This is the Italian version of the classic Austrian strudel dish with apples, raisins, and cinnamon. This regional recipe substitutes vegetables for the fruit, and the result is both healthy and delicious.

Serves 8

Heat the oil with 1 clove garlic in a large, nonstick frying pan over medium heat. Add the zucchini slices, and season with ¼ teaspoon salt and ¼ teaspoon pepper. Stir well and cook for 5 minutes until the zucchini begins to brown. Add the broth, cover with a lid, reduce the heat to medium-low, and cook for 10 minutes more.

Remove the lid and cook another 5 minutes, until all zucchini are tender and some of the broth has evaporated. Use a slotted spoon to remove the zucchini and set aside to cool. Discard the remaining liquid.

Put the carrot slices into a heavy saucepan along with the butter, 1 clove garlic, ¼ teaspoon salt, ¼ teaspoon pepper, sugar, and ½ cup water. Cover and cook over medium heat for 25 minutes, or until the carrots are tender. Remove from heat and set aside to cool.

Preheat the oven to 375 degrees F.

On a floured board or countertop, roll the pastry dough out into a 10 x 15-inch rectangle.

Line a baking sheet with parchment paper and place the pastry on it. Cover the center length of the pastry (leave about 2 inches of pastry at the bottom and the top) with a layer of fontina, then half of the carrots, and then half of the Gruyere and Gorgonzola. Cover the cheeses with the zucchini and sprinkle with the remaining Gruyere and Gorgonzola. Cover with the remaining carrots and sprinkle the whole thing with Parmigiano-Reggiano cheese.

Fold the pastry dough over the filling, pinching the sides together to seal well. Fold the ends together also and pinch to close. Dilute the beaten egg yolk with 1 teaspoon water and brush over the top of the strudel.

Bake for 45 minutes, or until golden brown. Remove from oven, transfer to a serving dish, and serve hot, cut into slices.

INGREDIENTS

2 tablespoons extra virgin olive oil

2 cloves garlic, divided

½ pound (about 2 to 3) baby zucchini, cut into ¼-inch rounds

½ teaspoon salt, divided

½ teaspoon black pepper, divided

⅓ cup vegetable broth

¾ pound carrots (about 3 medium), peeled and cut into ¼ inch rounds

2 tablespoons unsalted butter

1 teaspoon sugar

9 ounces frozen pastry dough, thawed

1 ounce fontina cheese, thinly sliced

1 cup coarsely-grated Gruyere

½ cup crumbled Gorgonzola

2 tablespoons grated Parmigiano-Reggiano cheese

1 egg yolk

VITELLO TONNATO
Veal in Tuna Sauce

A summertime Italian favorite, Vitello Tonnato likely originated in the Piemonte region of Italy. This dish is served cold, so roast the meat the day before and refrigerate it overnight.

Serves 8

Preheat the oven to 375 degrees F.

Tie the roast with kitchen string, and dust lightly with flour on all sides.

Heat the oil in a medium ovenproof skillet with a lid over medium-high heat. Sauté the garlic for 1 to 2 minutes just to flavor the oil. Brown the roast on all sides. Remove the garlic cloves, lower the heat to medium, season the roast with salt and pepper, and add the wine. Cook 2 to 3 minutes to let the wine evaporate a little. Place dabs of butter on the meat, cover, and transfer the skillet to the oven to roast for 50 minutes. Check often to see if the liquid has evaporated, and baste with up to 1 cup broth as necessary. When the roast is cooked, remove and set aside to cool.

Cover and refrigerate overnight.

To make the sauce, place the drained tuna, anchovy paste, remaining 2 tablespoons vegetable broth, and 3 tablespoons capers in a food processor and process until creamy.

Place the mayonnaise into a medium bowl. Add the tuna mixture a little at a time, mixing it well with a rubber spatula.

When you are ready to serve, cut the cold veal roast into thin slices, about ¼-inch thick or thinner. Place the slices on a large serving platter, spread the tuna sauce over the meat, and garnish with the remaining 1 tablespoon capers.

INGREDIENTS

1½ pound veal roast

2 tablespoons all-purpose flour, plus more as needed

3 tablespoons extra virgin olive oil

1 clove garlic, peeled

1 teaspoon salt

¼ teaspoon black pepper

½ cup dry white wine

4 tablespoons unsalted butter, softened

1 cup plus 2 tablespoons vegetable broth, divided

1 (7-ounce) can tuna packed in olive oil, and drained

1 tablespoon anchovy paste

4 tablespoons capers, divided

½ cup mayonnaise

Opposite page: Tita's garden looking toward her cousin's home.

TIRAMISÙ

Often lauded as a Tuscan invention, tiramisù has now been claimed by the Friuli region as their original creation. The word "tiramisù" translates to "pick me up" due to its inclusion of invigorating espresso, and you may adjust the amount of espresso in the recipe to your personal taste. As a variation, try slices of sponge cake in place of ladyfingers.

Serves 12

Fill a small saucepan with 2 inches of water and bring to a simmer over medium-low heat.

Whisk the egg yolks and sugar together in a metal bowl that can sit safely on top of the saucepan. Place the bowl on the saucepan and cook for about 20 minutes, whisking occasionally, until a candy thermometer placed in the egg mixture reaches 160 degrees F.

While the eggs are cooking, combine the mascarpone, rum, and vanilla powder in the bowl of an electric mixer or a large bowl using a hand mixer. Beat until well combined.

Prepare an ice bath in a large bowl. When the eggs reach 160 degrees F, transfer the bowl of eggs from the heat to the ice bath and whisk the eggs for 1 to 2 minutes to cool.

Add the eggs to the mascarpone and beat on low for 1 minute or until there are no lumps. Do not overmix or the mascarpone will separate. Transfer the egg-mascarpone mixture to a large bowl, if using a mixer. Clean bowl of the mixer, add the heavy cream, and beat until soft peaks form. Use a spatula to fold the whipped cream into the egg-mascarpone mixture until well combined, being careful not to deflate the whipped cream.

Place the espresso or coffee in a pie plate or shallow dish. Dip the ladyfingers into the coffee on both sides and layer them on the bottom of a 9 x 13-inch baking dish. Once the bottom layer is complete, top with a layer of cream. Repeat layering with ladyfingers and cream until all ingredients have been used.

Refrigerate for at least 2 hours, or overnight, before serving. Sprinkle cocoa powder on top before cutting.

INGREDIENTS

8 egg yolks

2¼ cups powdered sugar

3½ cups mascarpone

¼ cup rum

1 pinch vanilla powder

2¼ cups heavy cream

about 2 cups espresso or strong coffee

about 36 ladyfingers, or substitute sponge cake

2 tablespoons unsweetened cocoa powder

CHAPTER 2

An Amalfi Afternoon
THE SOLIMENE FAMILY, CAMPANIA

THE STORY OF VIETRI BEGINS WITH THE SOLIMENE FAMILY

and their ceramic factory. Their whimsical and colorful handpainted creations were what so enchanted my mother, sister, and me that we felt inspired to start the company in 1983, and so we eagerly returned to the seaside town of Vietri sul Mare a few months after our initial trip to determine product designs, negotiate prices, and place orders. Little did I know that the Solimenes would become incredibly dear to me and would hold a prominent, special role in my life for nearly four decades.

Little did I know that the Solimenes would become incredibly dear to me and would hold a prominent, special role in my life for nearly four decades.

With more than a 100-year history of ceramic production, the Solimenes are known, respected, and admired across the world. When I came across the factory, the owner of the business and patriarch of the family was an incredible man named Don Vincenzo Solimene. Over the years, I had the great privilege of getting to know him and his family.

The title of "Don" is the highest honor bestowed upon Italian leaders. It is a distinction for a person who is admired and loved in the greatest way. I have never known anyone else in Italy who has ever been given that title—and Don Vincenzo truly embodied it. He was quiet yet clear in intention, calm yet determined, kind and loving, and a family man above all else. He had 10 children, and I felt like I was the eleventh.

Susan and Toni Solimene in Salerno, 2021.
Opposite page: The Solimene factory in Vietri sul Mare.

The Solimene factory is housed in a spectacular modernist structure that looks like towering, undulating ceramic waves. From the ground floor inside you can see straight up to the skylights 50 feet overhead. Internal balconies on the floors above overlook the central courtyard, and the building pulses with activity and life. Each ceramic piece is shaped, handpainted, fired, packaged, and shipped from within the walls of this building. Some of the Solimene family members reside in apartments on the upper levels. The factory's seemingly waving, fluid architecture echoes all the activity and creativity that lives and breathes inside, as it is

always full of artisans working, family members calling to each other from one floor to another, beloved pets snoozing on the staircases, and the strong, vibrant heartbeat of a close-knit family.

While the creations that came from Solimene were always magnificent, it was sometimes a challenge for the factory to create, pack, and ship as many pieces as our growing orders required. I have never been afraid of hard work, so I started traveling to Vietri sul Mare regularly to spend weeks at a time in their factory, packaging up our orders item by item to ship to the US.

Over the years, I saw celebrities stop in to shop (photographing the family

Lee with Don Vincenzo Solimene and his daughters Cinzia, Anna, Cristina, and Giovanna at the Solimene factory. Opposite page: Various stages in the process of creating VIETRI's Campagna Dinnerware collection.

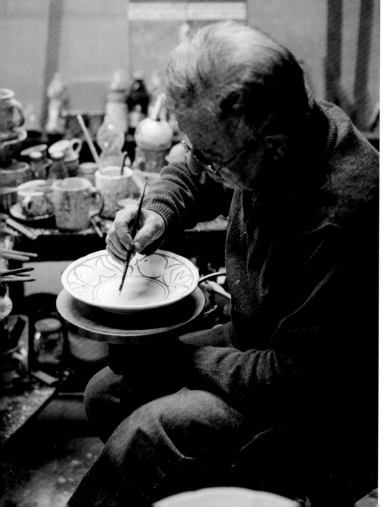

with Burt Reynolds was a highlight!), I cheered as the youngest Solimenes learned to walk and talk, and I watched thousands and thousands of dinner plates get painted with bright, cheerful designs.

I became familiar with the family rituals and dynamics: the distribution of a cappuccino or espresso to all the workers around 10 a.m. each morning, which grandchildren were likely to send plates crashing to the ground with a rambunctious game of chase, and who the most diligent bookkeepers were (always the daughters!). I noted that the entire family gathered upstairs every day for an hour to take a break and eat lunch together. I enjoyed a friendly relationship with the Solimenes, and I thought that they liked me, but a courteous, professional distance existed between them and anyone outside the family.

Therefore, it came as a great surprise and true honor when, after five years of traveling to and working in the Solimene factory, Don Vincenzo invited me to join the family for lunch. In all my time packing up VIETRI orders on the factory floor, I had never witnessed someone outside the Solimene family joining in their midday meal, and so I accepted the invitation with amazement and delight.

At the appointed hour, I excitedly, and a bit nervously, ascended the curving staircase to the family kitchen. Inside, I saw a huge square table topped with big bowls full of beautiful food prepared by Don Vincenzo's wife, Signora Vincenza Solimene, and her sisters-in-law. Twenty Solimene family members were gathered around the table, and they welcomed me to sit down.

Scenes from Tonino's terrace at the Solimene factory in Vietri sul Mare.

After thanking Signora Solimene and the sisters-in-law for their preparations and invitation, I sat down for the family meal, and any nerves I had experienced melted away as the family's relaxed conversations, genial joking, and boisterous banter began to fill the room.

Because Signora Solimene and her sisters-in-law cooked for a crowd every day, they had their menu perfected. Lunch included loaves of dense baguette torn into big hunks and dipped in olive oil, a light pasta, and a simply prepared fresh fish straight from that morning's boat trip. The big bowls were passed around family-style, and everyone helped themselves to generous portions. I remember feeling embraced in the family's warmth, history, and hospitality, and I tried my best to keep up with conversation (my Italian was still in its early days).

Lunch concluded with a light fruit dessert, caffè, and sometimes a little limoncello. The Solimenes taught me the process for making the intensely lemony, smooth, tart, sweet drink. I learned that authentic limoncello has a pale yellow color rather than the bright yellow-hued limoncellos you often see in gift shops.

Afterward, the crowd dispersed, some out to the aqua-tiled terrace overlooking the town and sea to enjoy a little sunshine, some retired to their rooms for a nap, some headed back to work, and the little ones returned to their play. With a family of 20, a business to run, and children to raise, everyone led full lives, but they all took the time to join together every day for lunch. To be included in this family ritual meant the world to me, and I did not take it for granted that first day, nor any day since when I have been invited back.

Since that first meal with them, I have rejoiced alongside the Solimenes as they welcomed new babies into the family. I have celebrated their family weddings. I grieved alongside them when their beloved patriarch, Don Vincenzo, passed away, and I have formed a wonderful relationship with the family's oldest son, Toni (Tonino) Solimene, the new head of the company and Vietri sul Mare's unofficial mayor. His lovely children are like dear grandchildren to me.

Sitting with the Solimenes for lunch that first time was the pivotal beginning of a deeper relationship with the family, and our personal and professional interests are now intertwined. Though we still haggle over delivery deadlines or missing products, it is done in the spirit of family, friendship, and a shared history. And we find that it is always easier to come to a happy compromise over a home-cooked lunch. May these favorite recipes of theirs become favorites in your family, too.

Don Vincenzo Solimene and Giuseppe Potenza. Opposite page: The garden dedicated to Don Vincenzo outside the Solimene factory.

MY FRIEND POTENZA

The first design I ever created for VIETRI was on September 2, 1983. I was with my sister, Frances, and our new agent, Fabio Puccinelli, in Vietri sul Mare at the Solimene factory. I described the exact design I wanted (a round, happy-looking fish) to their maestro artisan, Giuseppe Potenza, through hand movements and Fabio's translations. I thought his first name was Potenza back then because that is what I heard everyone call him. No one told me otherwise for 35 years. He did not care, nor did I. Somehow, we have always understood each other despite the language barrier.

Potenza is truly a maestro. In Italy, one becomes a maestro after working many years in their craft. The distinction is sometimes bestowed by the head of the factory and sometimes by the other painters. Potenza was recognized and respected as a maestro by everyone.

For almost 50 years, Potenza has sat down to paint in the same simple metal chair with a worn-out cushion. He is officially retired, yet still comes to work every day. This is what a maestro does. He loves his craft.

I cherished my time with Potenza. I would think of designs, bring new ideas, and gather plates he had designed in the past. We would take one element from one plate, another from another plate, and then we would play around with new color combinations. New ideas come from old ideas. That is design and creativity and honoring history. What a privilege it has been to create such beauty together.

As the years passed, Potenza's back began to hurt from sitting in his wobbly chair nine hours a day, six days a week. He told me he had heard of patches in the US that helped the pain. On my next visit, I brought him five boxes of Icy Hot pads. He loved them! On another trip, I brought a picture of the two of us together. His daughter recently told me that he keeps it in his living room.

Potenza came with Toni Solimene to the US one year to paint for a series of artisan events at Neiman Marcus and other top specialty stores. He had never visited this country. He was his usual humble, quiet self, but he warmed up as I translated and applauded his delicate brushstrokes. It was a trip neither of us will forget!

Today, Potenza is 75 years old. He looks great and still sits in the same chair in the same location at the factory. Whenever I go there, I search for him first. His hands and arms reach out. He has a big smile, and calls out, "Susanna!" My heart melts and we hug.

TAGLIOLINI AL FORNO
Baked Tagliolini

An easy pasta recipe to make ahead and reheat, this dish is perfect for large dinners. The combination of the creamy béchamel sauce with the ham, pasta, and peas makes a wonderfully satisfying dish.

Serves 8 to 10

Preheat the oven to 400 degrees F.

Cook the pasta per the package directions. Do not overcook. Drain. Prepare the béchamel sauce.

Transfer the cooked pasta to a large bowl along with the béchamel sauce, ham, peas, mozzarella, and pepper. Stir to combine.

Spread ½ cup breadcrumbs over the bottom of a 9 x 13-inch baking dish. Spread the pasta mixture evenly in the baking dish. Top with the remaining breadcrumbs and sprinkle the Parmigiano-Reggiano cheese evenly over the pasta.

Bake for 20 minutes and then broil for 10 minutes to crisp up the top.

INGREDIENTS

13 ounces tagliolini or fettuccine pasta

2 cups béchamel sauce (recipe, see page 62)

¾ cup diced ham

1 cup peas, cooked or frozen

8 ounces (1 cup) cubed mozzarella

Freshly ground black pepper, to taste

1 cup breadcrumbs, divided

1½ cups grated Parmigiano-Reggiano cheese

TORTA DI PUREA DI PATATE
Mashed Potato Pie

This entrée is infinitely adaptable, and it is a great way to use leftover mashed potatoes. Feel free to add extra ingredients like sliced hard-boiled eggs or cubed ham into the middle layer.

Serves 8

Preheat the oven to 350 degrees F.

Combine mashed potatoes, eggs, béchamel sauce, and 3 tablespoons grated cheese in a large bowl.

Butter a small baking dish and sprinkle with 2 tablespoons breadcrumbs. Place one layer of mashed potato mixture on the bottom of the casserole. Add a layer of mozzarella and then top with the remaining potato mixture. Sprinkle the remaining 2 tablespoons breadcrumbs and 3 tablespoons grated cheese atop the potatoes. Add the butter, cut into small pieces.

Bake for 30 to 40 minutes, until the top is bubbly and the edges are lightly browned.

INGREDIENTS

3 to 4 cups leftover mashed potatoes

2 eggs

2 cups béchamel sauce (recipe, see page 62)

6 tablespoons grated Parmigiano-Reggiano cheese, divided

2 tablespoons unsalted butter, plus more for buttering the baking dish

4 tablespoons breadcrumbs, divided

½ cup cubed mozzarella

BÉCHAMEL SAUCE

This classic sauce is one of the "mother" sauces in many different cuisines. The Italian version includes salt and nutmeg as a seasoning base. It is simple to make, but be careful not to burn the roux or the sauce will taste bitter.

Yields 2 cups

Heat the milk in a small saucepan over medium heat to just under a boil.

Meanwhile, in another medium saucepan, melt the butter over medium heat. Add the flour and stir 6 to 8 minutes until smooth to create a roux. The roux is done when it turns a light golden brown.

Once the roux has browned, lower the heat and whisk in the heated milk, about 1 cup at a time. Whisk constantly until all the milk is incorporated and the sauce is very smooth. Bring the mixture to a gentle boil over medium heat, then turn the heat to low and cook for 10 to 12 minutes, stirring constantly to prevent the sauce from burning on the bottom of the pan. The sauce is done when it is thick enough to coat the back of a spoon. Once done, remove from the heat and season with the salt and nutmeg.

INGREDIENTS

3 cups whole milk

5 tablespoons unsalted butter

¼ cup all-purpose flour

1½ teaspoons sea salt

½ teaspoon freshly grated nutmeg

CALAMARI RIPIENI
Stuffed Squid

Baked with a cheesy, peppery stuffing, these small squid are absolutely delicious. Squid are often available in large fish markets, but they can sometimes be difficult to find. In that case, ask your fishmonger if they can order it for you.

Serves 3 or 4

Cut the squid heads from the tentacles. Chop tentacles into small pieces. Set both aside.

Whisk the eggs in a medium bowl. Add the breadcrumbs, cheese, parsley, garlic, salt, and pepper. Stir to mix thoroughly. Set aside.

Heat 1 tablespoon olive oil in a small skillet over medium-low heat. Sauté the chopped tentacles until cooked, about 2 to 3 minutes, stirring to cook evenly. Let them cool sightly, then add the tentacles to the egg mixture and gently mix (you don't want the heat of the squid to cook the eggs).

Preheat the oven to 400 degrees F.

Use your fingers or a small spoon to fill the squid heads with the filling. Use a toothpick to secure each opening.

Use the remaining 1 tablespoon oil to grease the bottom of a baking dish. Nestle the squid inside the dish and bake for 20 minutes. Serve hot, with a salad or steamed vegetables.

INGREDIENTS

8 to 10 squid

2 eggs

1 cup breadcrumbs

2 tablespoons Parmigiano-Reggiano cheese

2 tablespoons chopped fresh Italian parsley

1 clove garlic, minced

½ teaspoon salt

¼ teaspoon black pepper

2 tablespoons extra virgin olive oil, divided

CHAPTER 3

The Young Man of Positano
GIOVANNI CARRASSI, CAMPANIA

GIOVANNI CARRASSI, OR THE MAYOR OF POSITANO AS I
affectionately refer to him, holds a dear place in my heart. I have been fortunate
enough to watch Giovanni grow from a vibrant young boy of three years old to
a brilliant, accomplished, kind gentleman and businessman. Following in the
footsteps of his grandmother and uncle before him, he now runs the family business,
Ceramica Assunta, where he sells bright, colorful, handpainted Italian ceramics
directly to delighted customers.

When I first met the Carrassi family, Ceramica Assunta was run by Giovanni's
uncle, Giuseppe Cinque. At that point, Ceramica Assunta was a second-generation
family business, as Giovanni's grandmother, Assunta, had opened the original shop
in Positano in 1948. The shop truly took off in 1970 when the famed Il San Pietro
Hotel opened and purchased its restaurant's dinnerware from Ceramica Assunta.
Like my mother, sister, and me, many of the hotel's guests were enchanted by the
hotel restaurant's colorful dinnerware, so the manager sent anyone interested in
making a purchase to Ceramica Assunta to buy pieces for their personal collections.

Giovanni and his parents lived in an apartment right above the store, so it isn't an
exaggeration to say that Giovanni ate, slept, and breathed ceramics from his earliest
days. I have vivid memories of Giovanni at five, six, and seven years old, racing
around the shop, helping his uncle with orders, and practicing his English with the

*Susan with Giovanni Carrassi,
his wife, Benedetta, son, Natale,
and daughter, Maria Teresa.
Opposite page: The terrace at
Giovanni's home, Villa Ferida.*

customers. Exuberant, friendly, and warmhearted, Giovanni has a charming personality that has stayed consistent to this day, and the business has become so successful that the Carrassi family now owns three ceramic shops in Positano.

With such an affable demeanor and rich history in Positano, it's no surprise that Giovanni seems to know everyone in town. It's impossible to stroll with him through the town's winding cobblestone streets without bumping into half a dozen dear friends of his, and through him I have met countless fascinating people from all walks of life. When his business allows, we take a midday break to enjoy lunch together, and he always takes me to the most delicious restaurants. Of course, Giovanni knows the chef in every restaurant, and he orders special items off the menu for us. While the food is simply prepared, the natural flavors are divine. From fresh-caught sea bass to sun-ripened tomatoes straight from the vine to warm loaves of bread right out of the oven, the food in Positano is unpretentious yet sublime. Never leave Positano without trying a pizza and calamari fritti!

Giovanni married a fantastic woman named Benedetta. They have two beautiful children, and one of my favorite sights in Positano is to see all four Carrassis loaded up on Giovanni's Vespa, zooming through town visiting friends and their various shops. I was particularly touched to hear of the family's generosity during the early days of the COVID-19 pandemic. Italy was hit hard, and Benedetta is a wonderful cook. She made over 150 small pizzas, and she and her family delivered them to the people around town who were

VIETRI's Pesci Colorati Dinnerware collection.

VILLA
FERIDA

confined to their homes and could not go out to buy food. She later repeated her kindness with a similar number of cake deliveries. I love the image of the whole family, weighed down with pizzas and cakes, spreading cheer and support throughout the seaside village.

Though Positano is one of the most celebrated travel destinations in the world, there is a friendly attitude and an effortless elegance that permeate the town. That spirit can also be seen in Giovanni and Benedetta's recent acquisition, the beautiful Villa Ferida. Filled with light and rich color, this airy villa was a lifelong dream for the family. They eventually hope to live there, but for now they rent it to others who come to this corner of the world for ocean views and a relaxed yet refined respite from daily life.

The Carrassis have been so kind as to share some of their favorite family recipes with me, and it's my honor to share them with you as well. I wish Benedetta could prepare them and deliver them to you via scooter, but until that's possible, I hope you can recreate them in your own kitchen and feel some of southern Italy's *la dolce vita* in your home, too.

Glimpses of Villa Ferida, located on the cliffs of Southern Italy's Amalfi Coast.

FIORI DI ZUCCA RIPIENI
Stuffed Zucchini Flowers

Zucchini flowers can be found fresh at Italian markets when they are in season in the spring. They are sold in beautiful bunches with the leaves attached. They are fragile, so handle gently and be sure your oil is hot so that they cook quickly.

Serves 4 to 6

Clean the zucchini flowers gently in cold water. Remove all stems around the outside of each flower and gently remove each interior stem.

To prepare the filling, combine the mozzarella, ricotta, basil, Parmigiano-Reggiano, salt, and pepper in a medium bowl. Adjust seasonings to taste.

Fill each zucchini flower with the cheese filling and gently twist the ends of the flower to close. Set aside.

Heat 2 inches of oil in a medium skillet over medium-high heat until a thermometer reads 350 degrees F.

Place the flour in a bowl. Place the beaten eggs in a separate bowl, and put the breadcrumbs on a plate.

Coat each stuffed flower in the flour, gently shaking off any excess. Then dip in the egg, and finally coat with the breadcrumbs until fully covered. Shake off any excess crumbs.

Gently lay a few flowers in the hot oil, being careful not to overcrowd the pan. Fry 2 to 3 minutes until golden, turning as needed to cook evenly. Remove to a paper towel-lined platter. Repeat until all flowers are fried.

Season with sea salt, basil, and cheese, as desired. Serve hot.

INGREDIENTS

12 zucchini flowers

2 cups chopped fresh mozzarella, drained of any liquid

2½ cups ricotta

Several leaves fresh basil, torn into small pieces

½ cup grated Parmigiano-Reggiano cheese

1 teaspoon salt, plus additional to taste

¼ teaspoon black pepper, plus additional to taste

Peanut or sunflower oil

1 cup all-purpose flour, or more as needed

2 eggs, beaten

1 cup breadcrumbs, or more as needed to cover each flower

Optional garnishes: sea salt, basil, more Parmigiano-Reggiano cheese

POLPETTE
Meatballs

Meatballs are beloved in all of Italy, as they are in the US. Italians love to serve them alone, as seen here. They are also wonderful atop a serving of buttered linguine. These are some of the best meatballs I have ever tasted.

Yields 22 to 32, depending on size

Preheat oven to 400 degrees F.

In a large mixing bowl, combine the breadcrumbs, ground beef, egg, garlic, cheese, salt, pepper, and parsley. Mix with your hands until well combined.

Form meatballs to the size you prefer, either golf ball-sized or smaller. Place some flour in a bowl or saucer and dust the meatballs lightly with flour.

Arrange the meatballs on a lightly-oiled rimmed baking sheet. Bake for 15 minutes, turning halfway through, until the meatballs are evenly browned and a meat thermometer placed in a meatball reads 165 degrees F. Serve immediately.

INGREDIENTS

2 cups breadcrumbs

2 pounds lean ground beef

1 egg

3 cloves garlic, minced

4 cups grated Parmigiano-Reggiano cheese

1 teaspoon salt, or more to taste

½ teaspoon black pepper, or more to taste

1 bunch fresh Italian parsley, leaves chopped

All-purpose flour, for dusting

Peanut, canola, or olive oil

GNOCCHI AL LIMONE
Gnocchi in Lemon Sauce

Italian 00 flour, also known as doppio zero, is a super-fine flour used for making pasta and pizza dough. It can be found at most grocery stores, Italian specialty markets, or online. This recipe makes a large quantity, but it freezes beautifully. To freeze, place the uncooked gnocchi between layers of wax paper sprayed with cooking oil or spread them onto cookie sheets, then cover with plastic wrap and freeze. You can store the frozen gnocchi in a plastic zip top bag in the freezer for up to 6 weeks.

Yields about 7 dozen

To make the gnocchi, boil the whole potatoes with the skins on for approximately 20 to 25 minutes, depending on the size. The potatoes are done when you can easily slice them in half. Drain and set aside to cool. When cool enough to handle, peel and mash or put the potatoes through a ricer.

In a large bowl, place the potatoes, egg, flour, and salt and thoroughly combine.

Dust your countertop or work surface with a little flour. Being careful not to overwork the dough, bring it together, form it into a flat round and cut into four quarters. Take one-fourth of the dough and roll into a long rope-like shape, about ½-inch thick. Cut into ½-inch pieces.

To give the gnocchi its signature ridges, you can either use a gnocchi board, or flour the tines of a fork and place the fork tines side down on the countertop. Press each gnocchi into the tines, then use your thumb to roll the gnocchi off the tines. Repeat the process with all portions of the dough, and flour the fork again when the gnocchi sticks.

Bring water to a boil in a medium saucepan over high heat. When water boils, drop some of the gnocchi in the water without overcrowding. Boil for 2 to 3 minutes, or until the gnocchi float. Set a colander over a paper towel-lined plate. Remove the cooked gnocchi with a slotted spoon to the colander to drain. Repeat until all the gnocchi you plan to serve are cooked. Freeze any extra gnocchi for future meals.

INGREDIENTS

For the gnocchi:

2 pounds Yukon Gold potatoes

1 egg

1¾ cups Italian 00 flour, plus more for dusting work surface

1 teaspoon salt

For the sauce:

8 tablespoons unsalted butter

¾ cup heavy cream

Zest of 2 lemons, divided

Salt, to taste

Optional garnishes: grated Parmigiano-Reggiano, freshly ground black pepper

To make the sauce, combine the butter, cream, and zest from 1 lemon in a sauté pan over medium-low heat. Bring to a simmer and cook for 5 minutes, or until the cream reduces.

Add the cooked gnocchi to the sauce and toss for 1 minute. Season with salt and the remaining zest to taste. Serve with grated cheese and pepper.

MELANZANE ALLA PARMIGIANA
Eggplant Parmesan

This recipe for the American/Italian favorite is failproof because it calls for the eggplant to be sautéed before it is baked. This extra step ensures that it will have a tasty, tender bite rather than being tough. Make sure to sweat the eggplant slices before you sauté them so there is no taste of bitterness.

Serves 12

Trim the eggplant and cut lengthwise into thin slices. Place the sliced eggplant on a plate and sprinkle both sides with salt. Allow to sit for 30 minutes. After 30 minutes, rinse the eggplant with water and pat dry.

Heat 1 cup oil in a large skillet over medium-high heat. Place the flour in a shallow bowl and coat each eggplant slice in flour. Fry 2 to 3 minutes per side until golden. Transfer to a paper towel-lined baking sheet to drain. Repeat until all eggplant is cooked.

Preheat the oven to 350 degrees F.

Spoon a portion of the tomato sauce on the bottom of a 9 x 13-inch baking dish. Then layer with the eggplant, then the mozzarella cubes, and then another portion of the tomato sauce. Sprinkle with salt and pepper.

Create two to three more layers. Finish with the tomato sauce and top with the grated cheese.

Bake for 35 to 40 minutes, until the top is bubbling and golden.

Remove from the oven and let the casserole rest for 5 to 10 minutes to cool slightly. Garnish with fresh basil, if desired. Serve immediately and pass the extra Parmigiano-Reggiano cheese around the table.

INGREDIENTS

4 medium eggplant (about 4½ pounds)

4 cups sunflower oil or peanut oil, divided

1½ cups flour, plus more as needed

1½ cups tomato sauce

1 pound fresh mozzarella, chopped in small cubes

Salt and black pepper, to taste

½ cup grated Parmigiano-Reggiano cheese, plus more for the table

Optional garnish: fresh basil

RAVIOLI CAPRESI
Capri-Style Ravioli

Amazingly good, these vegetarian ravioli are perfect little pockets of ricotta and mozzarella in a sauce made from vine-ripened tomatoes. It is worth the effort to make your own ravioli, so don't be afraid to try even if you don't have a pasta machine.

Yields about 6 dozen

Combine both flours and form a mound on the countertop. Create a well in the center.

Beat nine eggs and place them into the well. Slowly mix with a fork, pulling flour from the outside of the well until the flour begins to hold together. Dust your hands with flour and mix gently; you are aiming for a soft, smooth dough. Cover the dough with plastic wrap or a tea towel, and let it sit for 30 minutes at room temperature.

To prepare the filling, combine the ricotta, mozzarella, basil, salt, and pepper in a medium bowl. Stir until fully combined and set aside.

When the dough has rested, transfer it to a floured surface and divide into 4 portions. Roll out one portion of the dough with a rolling pin or a pasta machine into thin, rectangular sheets. Keep 00 flour within reach; you will need to flour the machine, rolling pin, hands, and dough from time to time.

Fold the sheet of dough in half and then unfold creating a crease down the middle of the pasta. Brush one side of the pasta with the remaining beaten egg. Add teaspoons of the filling in a row about 1-inch apart on the side of the pasta sheet brushed with egg. Fold the other side over to cover the filling, making sure to press out any air pockets. Cut the ravioli using a round cutter or a knife. Using the tines of a fork, press the outer edges together to ensure the filling does not leak during boiling.

Bring salted water to a boil over medium-high heat in a large stockpot and cook the ravioli in batches for 1 to 2 minutes, until they float. Drain and set aside.

INGREDIENTS

2½ cups Italian 00 flour

1 cup finely ground Semola "Rimacinata" flour

10 eggs, divided

2 cups ricotta

1½ cups cubed fresh mozzarella

2 tablespoons minced fresh basil

½ teaspoon salt, plus more to taste

¼ teaspoon freshly ground black pepper, plus more to taste

3 tablespoons olive oil

2 cloves garlic

4 cups tomato purée

2 tablespoons chopped fresh basil

1 cup heavy cream

Optional garnish: grated Parmigiano-Reggiano cheese

To prepare the sauce, heat 3 tablespoons olive oil in a large heavy-bottomed saucepan over medium heat. Add the garlic and sauté for 2 to 3 minutes. Add the tomato purée and fresh basil and sauté for 10 to 15 minutes. Add the cream and season to taste with salt and pepper.

Increase heat to high and toss ravioli in sauce for 30 seconds just before serving.

Serve immediately with grated Parmigiano-Reggiano cheese.

PESCE ALL'ACQUA PAZZA
Fish in Crazy Water

An alternative to baking or frying, cooking the fish in a little water results in a tender, flaky fish along with a tasty broth. Plate in shallow bowls or rimmed plates, spoon the vegetables on top of each piece of fish, and serve with crusty bread to soak any leftover broth.

Serves 4

Heat the olive oil in a large lidded skillet over medium heat. Add the garlic, onion, and celery, and sauté for 3 to 5 minutes, stirring occasionally. Add the tomatoes, olives, capers, and parsley, and stir to combine.

Place the filets on top of the vegetables and sprinkle each filet with salt. Add enough water to the skillet to cover the vegetables, but make sure it only reaches the bottom of the filets.

Cover tightly and cook for 10 to 15 minutes until fish is fully cooked and flakes easily. Serve hot.

INGREDIENTS

⅔ cup extra virgin olive oil

1 clove garlic, smashed

1 medium onion, diced

3 stalks celery, diced

1 pint cherry tomatoes, cut in half

½ cup pitted, halved kalamata olives

¼ cup capers

1 tablespoon minced Italian parsley leaves

3 to 4 white fish filets, such as flounder, sea bass, or sea bream

½ teaspoon salt

TORTA CAPRESE
Almond Chocolate Cake

Italians generally prefer cakes without glazes or icing, and the cakes are typically enjoyed at lunch as well as in the mid-afternoon with an espresso.

Serves 10 to 12

Preheat the oven to 350 degrees F.

Line a springform pan with parchment paper, and butter the bottom and the sides of the paper.

Place the chocolate and butter together in top of a double boiler and bring to a simmer over medium heat. If you do not have a double boiler, add 1 inch of water to a small saucepan and set a metal mixing bowl atop the pan. Stir until the chocolate and butter are melted and combined. Pull off heat and let cool.

In the bowl of a standing mixer, or using a hand mixer, whip the egg whites 6 to 8 minutes until stiff peaks form.

In a large mixing bowl, whisk the egg yolks and sugar until well creamed. Stir in the almond flour and add the chocolate mixture slowly, stirring until fully combined. Stir in the all-purpose flour and baking powder. Carefully fold the whipped egg whites into the cake batter so as not to deflate them.

Pour the batter into the cake pan and level the top. Bake for 40 to 45 minutes until a toothpick inserted in the center comes out clean. Cool before serving. Sprinkle with powdered sugar.

INGREDIENTS

1 cup (2 sticks) plus 6 tablespoons butter, plus more for buttering pan

10 ounces bittersweet chocolate

6 eggs, separated

1⅓ cups sugar

2½ cups almond flour

1 cup all-purpose flour

2 teaspoons baking powder

Optional garnish: ½ cup powdered sugar whipped cream

A STROLL THROUGH POSITANO

It has been 40 years since my first visit to Positano, and while its winding streets, charming shops, and colorful cliffside buildings are now as familiar to me as a lifelong friend, the town still takes my breath away every time. Here are a few of my favorite places to visit when I am in town; I hope you will visit and enjoy them as I do.

IL SAN PIETRO DI POSITANO: This extraordinary hotel was built by Carlo Cinque, a straw-hatted, linen-suited, lovely gentleman who first built the villa for himself and then turned the magnificent piece of architecture into a wonder for others to enjoy.

HOTEL PALAZZO MURAT: As you stroll down the cobblestone path to the marina, you will come across this beautiful hotel. I painted my home's front doors in honor of its ochre doors! The bar is peaceful, and the outside garden offers a perfect place to have a caffè, prosecco, or limoncello.

LA FENICE: A wonderful, small hotel perched on the hillside overlooking the sea about a seven-minute walk from Positano. Small bungalows are on the lower side of the street, and the main house and breakfast area are above the street. Bougainvillea, grape, and lemon vines create a delicious scent along the walkways.

LA SPONDA: This Michelin star restaurant in the Hotel Le Sirenuse is situated on a patio overlooking the village and the sea. Euphoric! The hotel is a former villa filled with antiques and linen and silk fabrics, and it is oh so-casually elegant. It also has one of chicest shops inside the main reception, as well as across the street.

TRATTORIA LA TAGLIATA: A relaxed trattoria in the hills of Positano Alto, this restaurant is run by a wonderful family of third-generation Positaneans. There is no menu—you eat what they bring you, and it is out of this world. *A must!*

TRE SORELLE: At the base of the town, this restaurant has a beautiful view of the sea. A fresh Margherita pizza, a glass of vino bianco secco, and maybe an insalata verde con olio d'oliva—the perfect menu in my opinion. End the meal with limoncello: so cold, so heavenly.

TRE DENARI: My go-to shoe store for leather or suede loafers and sandals. The owner, Maurizio, is delightful and has been in the same spot for years.

LA BOTTEGA DI BRUNELLI: Visit this gorgeous shop for dressier clothes. Two of my favorite pieces in my wardrobe were purchased here—a fabulous pair of teal trousers and a top with tiny pleats.

PROFUMI DI POSITANO: My favorite *profumeria* ever! Situated on a small road, Via C. Colombo, leading out of Positano, this tiny bottega uses only natural ingredients, including their own lemons. The scents are clean and as fresh as the seaside air. Giuseppe and Giuseppina present beautifully packaged air fresheners, soaps, and perfumes to fill every visitor's memory of their visit to Positano. It is a favorite gift to take home.

CERAMICA ASSUNTA: *I cannot resist!* The most beautiful handpainted ceramics you will ever see for your home and garden can be found here. This is Giovanni's family shop, and they have three locations in Positano. They ship all over the world and can custom design anything your heart desires.

SAPORI DI POSITANO: My favorite shop for all things lemon! Here you will find lemon jams, biscuits, candies, honey, and my favorite, lemon chocolates.

CHAPTER 4

Tuscan Hidden Treasures

FRANCO AMMANNATI, TUSCANY

PERHAPS THE QUICKEST WAY TO DESCRIBE MY DEAR, smiling, kindhearted friend Franco Ammannati is that my nickname for him is "Franco Mio" or "My Franco." Everyone who meets him is captivated by his warmth and good humor, and our friendship has been one of the buoys of my life.

I saw it—the warm color of Tuscan wheat, the rich red earth, the fresh green trees, and the creamy white of the clouds.

I first met Franco in the mid-1990s while walking the gift show in Frankfurt, Germany. I came upon a booth of a factory I had never seen before called Ceramiche Virginia. Among all the items they were selling, I saw a gold-foiled ceramic votive. It was simple with clean, classic lines. VIETRI was selling lots of dinnerware, but we did not have candleholders. I knew gold would go with anything, so I thought we should try it. That fall, we introduced the votives for the holiday season, and they were an immediate hit. Little did I know at the time that our partnership with Ceramiche Virginia would become incredibly successful and long-lasting.

Franco was Ceramiche Virginia's master designer, and we instantly hit it off. I came to visit him and the factory during one business trip, and after a full morning of work, Franco took me to the nearby town of Poppi for lunch (one of Franco's

Susan and Franco with chef Francesco Pieraccioli at his family's restaurant, La Lanterna. Opposite page: The Tuscan fields that inspired VIETRI's Cucina Fresca Dinnerware collection.

most prominent characteristics is his love of good food and a proper lunch every day at 1 p.m. on the dot).

In Tuscany, Poppi is known for its magnificent 13th-century castle and stunning views of the Casentino Valley. We had a long lunch of pasta and sliced pork with wine in the afternoon glow of the Tuscan town. Franco never orders off a menu—he seems to know every chef in Italy and routinely goes into the kitchen to ask him or her to prepare something special.

I told Franco that I wanted to create a unique, solid color dinnerware collection. We talked through color possibilities, but it wasn't until our stroll across a bridge that the scenery, situation, and sunlight struck me. And then, looking out over the valley below us, I saw it—the warm color of Tuscan wheat, the rich red earth, the fresh green trees, and the creamy white of the clouds—these colors of Tuscany were exactly what I wanted to emulate on the dinnerware. Franco understood and got to work.

About two months later, I received a call from Franco. *"Fatto!" (It's done!)*, he proudly exclaimed. I went back to Italy soon after to see what Franco and the artisans had been working on. I walked into a room filled with about 250 samples in different shapes and in

the Tuscan colors we had discussed. It was truly one of the pivotal moments of my life. I was utterly blown away! Franco's creations completely captured the feeling of Tuscany, with its rich yet soft colors, organic shapes, and rustic edges.

Franco had found a Renaissance painting featuring peasants using simple earthenware plates fired in their own bread ovens. Because the peasants' materials and techniques were primitive, the glazes would separate from the edges of the plates after firing. Franco and the artisans mimicked this rustic look by painting wax around the edges of each piece, causing a bit of the earthenware to peek through during firing, a look that is now copied the world over. This was it! Simple and iconic. And it ended up starting an entire trend in US home design. It felt like a worthy tribute to the Tuscan region I loved, and still love, so much.

When I asked Franco what we should name this collection, his suggestion was Cucina Fresca for Fresh Kitchen. That was the beginning of what would be the most popular and widely sold dinnerware in VIETRI's history. We even won an American Design Award for it. Cucina Fresca grew into a collection of more than 10 colors and 35 accessories over the years.

Our next venture with Franco's factory was the best-selling Lastra collection. Once again, it was designed taking parts of the past with innovations for today. It is modeled and named after an antique wooden strap used for cheesemaking throughout Italy. Franco's designs resonate with the world while honoring the essence of his Tuscan home.

Speaking of home, Franco often invites me over to dine when I visit. He has a small kitchen from which he makes magic. Always cooking what's in season, Franco relies on the highest quality ingredients to do the heavy lifting of his recipes. There is a little bottega just down the street from his house, and he pops in every day to pick up fresh vegetables, breads,

Scenes from La Lanterna.
Opposite page: Cucina Fresca, one of VIETRI's first and most beloved dinnerware collections.

cheeses, and sliced meats. Like many Italians, he is of the belief that one should keep recipes simple and allow nature's flavors to sing. We've now become close enough that Franco allows me to help him prepare the meal, and we always have a great time puttering around the kitchen, with him giving me very clear instructions and straightforward jobs so I avoid messing up things!

When he is not dining in his own home, you can be sure to find Franco dining at his home-away-from-home, Ristorante La Lanterna. Ristorante La Lanterna and the Pieraccioli family have been a huge part of my 40-year Tuscan journey. On Via di Pulica in the Tuscan hills above Florence, La Lanterna has been my go-to restaurant since Franco took me for the first time in the mid-1980s. Francesco, the chef and owner, is the fourth generation of Pieracciolis and a close friend

to Franco. His parents, the third generation and former owners, are still at the restaurant daily, helping wherever they can lend a hand. Mamma e Babbo (Mom and Dad, as I call them) are always happy to see me when I return, and they pat my cheeks with glee as if I am a grandchild. Every server welcomes me back with a wave and a smile, and it is not unusual for us to be treated to a taste of the current freshest vegetable dish or a dessert just prepared as soon as we sit down.

Franco and I usually have a typical Tuscan lunch of mixed bruschetta, a homemade pasta dish, and fried mushrooms, or mixed fried meats with a salad. This is always with La Lanterna's own olive oil as well as their own wine. We either come alone or with some others from the factory to discuss new designs or current challenges. We see old friends and meet new ones. Franco always knows

Antipasti at La Lanterna.
Opposite page: Susan with the
Pieraccioli family.

someone at the restaurant and makes introductions all around. I have made new vendor relationships through Franco there even during the most casual of lunches. Our conversations are always filled with laughter, and at the end we toast to how lucky we are to work together and be friends.

Franco and I have also shared many memorable times together in the US. Franco once came to do a series of artisan events, and he was scheduled to do a signing at A Southern Season, a fabulous gourmet food and gift store in Chapel Hill. The store had a well-known cooking school, and once they learned that Franco was coming to visit, they asked if he would lead a cooking class. He excitedly agreed, and the course sold out in less than two days. Franco doesn't speak much English, so I agreed to go with him and serve as the translator in front of the class.

I was familiar with the recipes, and my Italian was decent by this point, but once Franco went on stage and started explaining all the intricacies of every ingredient and step in each recipe, I was a bit out of my depth. Franco would give a nuanced and lengthy explanation of exactly how to julienne a carrot at a certain angle and with a certain finesse, and all I could manage was "cut your carrot!" The fact that my English translations lasted about a tenth as long as his Italian instructions brought the audience great laughter, and our cooking show turned into a bit of a comedy performance as well. Luckily, everyone ended up with a delicious meal, and A Southern Season gave Franco a standing invitation to come back to teach whenever he could.

Franco has now retired, but he continues to help VIETRI build new vendor relationships. Additionally, I am reminded of his joyful spirit throughout the day in my dog, funnily enough! My husband, Bill, and I decided to get a puppy a few years back, and when it was time to pick our new family member from the litter, we were both delighted by a little one who played his heart out and then retreated to the edge of the room to take a good nap on his own. This friendly, contented spirit reminded us so much of our dear friend Franco that we called the Italian Franco to see if he would mind having an American namesake. When Franco heard that his namesake would be a dog, he said, in his typical good humor, "Oh, even better!" Whenever I see our dog Franco trotting happily toward me or enjoying a well-deserved rest in the sun, I'm reminded of Franco Ammannati, my wonderful friend of so many years who has taught me to appreciate the beauty and deliciousness of the world around me.

I hope that Franco's recipes do the same for you, and that they bring the warmth and the genuine nature of Tuscany into your home as well.

Clockwise from top: The wine menu at La Lanterna; The Duomo in Florence, Italy; Francesco Cafaggi, Franco's godson and chef at La Lanterna.
Opposite page: The cantina at La Lanterna.

101

Susan with the Pieraccioli family and staff at La Lanterna.

BRUSCHETTA CON POMODORI
Bruschetta with Tomatoes

Bruschetta can be topped with any kind of tomato to add color and vibrance. Olives are used to top the bruschetta in regions like Puglia, Sicily, Campagna, and Tuscany. Pine nuts and oregano are a wonderful addition as well.

Serves 4 (2 per person)

Combine the tomatoes, salt, pepper, oregano, basil, and olive oil in a medium bowl. Stir to fully combine. Taste and add more salt and pepper if needed. You can make this dish earlier in the day and chill until you are ready to serve.

When you are ready to serve, toast 8 slices of bread and spread the mixture on top.

INGREDIENTS

3 ripe medium tomatoes, diced

¼ teaspoon salt

12 grinds black pepper, or to taste

¼ teaspoon dried oregano

1 tablespoon chopped fresh basil leaves

2 tablespoons extra virgin olive oil

8 slices good Italian bread

POMODORI E MOZZARELLA
Tomatoes and Mozzarella

This salad is classic, simple, and absolutely wonderful with the freshest of ingredients. It's no wonder that the colors of the Italian flag are red, green, and white!

Serves 4

Arrange the tomatoes and mozzarella on a serving platter. Sprinkle with the green olives. Drizzle with olive oil. Sprinkle with salt and pepper to taste, and garnish with basil and celery leaves.

INGREDIENTS

4 medium tomatoes, sliced

1 pound fresh mozzarella, sliced

¼ cup sliced green olives

2 tablespoons extra virgin olive oil

1 teaspoon sea salt

¼ teaspoon freshly ground black pepper

Handful fresh basil leaves

Handful fresh celery leaves

RIBOLLITA
Tuscan Bread Soup

If you cannot find Tuscan kale, also known as dinosaur kale, you may substitute half a small head of green cabbage, chopped into bite-size pieces. This is a heart-healthy soup with the addition of vitamin-packed cannellini beans and vegetables. Delicious!

Serves 12 to 14

Combine the cannellini beans, garlic, and sage in a stock pot or Dutch oven. Cover with water by about 2 inches and simmer for 2 hours, or until tender. Add more water as needed. Once beans are tender, drain and set aside.

Heat the olive oil in the Dutch oven over medium-low heat. Sauté the onion and zucchini 3 to 5 minutes, until slightly browned. Add the potato, carrots, celery, chard leaves, kale, cooked beans, and 12 cups water. Bring to a low boil, then lower the heat and simmer for about 3 hours. Add water during cooking if the soup dries out too much. Stir in salt, pepper, and tomato paste. Taste and adjust seasoning as necessary.

Place a handful of the bite-sized bread pieces in the bottom of each bowl. Top with soup and serve with Parmesan cheese, or pass the cheese around the table.

INGREDIENTS

2¾ cups dried cannellini beans

2 cloves garlic

1 sprig fresh sage

3 tablespoons extra virgin olive oil

1 medium onion, diced (about 1 cup)

1 large zucchini, halved and sliced (about 2 cups)

1 russet potato, peeled and cut into ½-inch cubes

1 carrot, peeled and sliced

2 celery ribs, sliced

6 chard leaves, stems removed, leaves chopped

6 Tuscan kale leaves, stems removed, leaves chopped

1 teaspoon salt

½ teaspoon black pepper

1 to 2 tablespoons tomato paste

4 to 6 slices stale, rustic bread, torn into bite-size pieces

Optional garnish: ½ cup grated Parmigiano-Reggiano cheese

LONZA DI MAIALE CON PISELLI
Pork Loin with Peas

This makes a great presentation for a special dinner, and it's simple to make. Be sure to check the pork every 20 minutes so that you don't overcook. When your meat thermometer reads 145 degrees F, it is done. You want the meat to be slightly pink inside. As it rests, it will release the au jus you can use when serving.

Serves 4

Preheat oven to 350 degrees F.

Season the pork loin with salt and pepper. Use a small knife to make holes in the pork and insert a garlic clove into each hole.

Tie rosemary sprigs to the outside of the pork using kitchen string.

Drizzle oil to cover the bottom of a baking dish, place the pork loin in it, and roast for 1 to 1½ hours, or until the internal temperature reaches 145 degrees F. Use a meat thermometer to check the temperature of the meat after 60 minutes.

When it is done, remove from the oven and let it rest for 10 minutes before slicing. While the pork rests, either steam the peas for 1 to 2 minutes or boil for 2 to 3 minutes.

Drain before serving. Slice the pork and serve with the peas and garnish with a sprig of rosemary.

INGREDIENTS

3 pounds pork loin
or pork tenderloin

1 teaspoon salt

¼ teaspoon black pepper

6 cloves garlic, peeled

6 sprigs rosemary

1 tablespoon
extra virgin olive oil

2 cups fresh green peas

BISCOTTINI ARANCE E PINOLI
Orange and Pine Nut Biscottini

Bustina di lievito per dolci is an Italian baking powder used for desserts. It is available online or in specialty grocery stores. You may also substitute two teaspoons of baking powder and a pinch of vanilla powder. These cookies are best when prepared the day before you plan to serve them.

Yields about 30

Preheat oven to 350 degrees F.

Line a rimmed baking sheet with parchment paper and set aside.

Place the flour, sugar, and Italian baking powder in a large bowl. Add the eggs and stir to combine. Add the pine nuts and olive oil and stir to combine. Add the zest and 1 tablespoon orange juice and stir until the dough comes together. If the dough is crumbly, add 1 more tablespoon juice.

Sprinkle flour on a countertop or work surface. Turn out the dough onto the floured surface and divide it into two equal parts.

Using your hands, roll each into logs about 2-inches thick and 8-inches long. Place on the lined baking sheet.

Bake for 25 minutes until the top is a golden color. Remove and set the logs aside on a cooling rack for 1 hour.

Use a serrated knife to slice into ¾-inch thick cookies. Remove the parchment and place the cookies on the baking sheet to cool overnight.

The next day, preheat the oven to 350 degrees F. Bake the cookies on the baking sheet for 10 minutes, then use a spatula to turn them, and bake another 10 minutes. Let them cool completely before serving.

INGREDIENTS

2 cups all-purpose flour

1 cup sugar

1 (16 gram) packet bustina di lievito per dolci, or 2 teaspoons baking powder with a pinch of vanilla powder

2 eggs

½ cup shelled pine nuts

1 teaspoon olive oil

Zest of 1 orange

1 to 2 tablespoons orange juice

CERAMICHE VIRGINIA

Ceramiche Virginia was founded in 1971 in Montespertoli, a village perched on a beautiful hillside outside of Florence. The business is named for the small nearby Virginia River. During the past 50 years, it has weathered industry challenges, enjoyed incredible successes, and stayed fresh and forward-looking. I feel lucky to have discovered the company early on in VIETRI's journey, as our partnership with them has brought about some of our most successful collections and great joy to many families.

Maestro artisan Stefano Roselli is officially retired but continues to lead Ceramiche Virginia's design process. Born in 1957 on the outskirts of Florence, Stefano began his creative career in a local candle factory at the age of 14. There, he honed his skills for both molding and casting before transitioning to ceramics. Creative, innovative, and passionate, Stefano quickly fell in love with the details and nuances achieved by various clays and was deemed a maestro molder in 1989. As Stefano oversees the design and creative processes for all ceramics produced in the factory, he also mentors his protégé, Cristian Massaro.

Stefano took inspiration from a circular wooden slab used for cheesemaking found at a local antiques market to create molds for the Lastra collection, now celebrating more than 10 years in production and a current VIETRI bestseller. The wooden hoop, held together with twine, was left with a slight overlap to help maintain the shape of the cheese mold. Stefano incorporates this overlapping detail into the entire design of Lastra dinnerware and accessories, from foot to rim, creating clean and simple lines. A dark dusting on the edges of each piece suggests the ash that was used to preserve these cheeses and highlights each unique silhouette.

A true artist, Stefano's work is also his passion. He is most at home when he has clay on his hands and sketches for possible designs scattered across his workspace. During his free time, he sculpts Renaissance and Roman-inspired bas-reliefs in his home workshop and enjoys an occasional and much-deserved glass of La Caccia Rosso.

Clockwise from top: Bill and Susan with the team at Ceramiche Virginia: Stefano Roselli, Amerigo Coli, Franco Ammannati, and Mirko Pucci; An artisan adds a dark dusting to the edge of a pasta bowl from VIETRI's Lastra collection; Maestro artisan Stefano Roselli sculpts a piece of Lastra.

CHAPTER 5

A Home Away from Home
XENIA LEMOS, TUSCANY

ALTHOUGH IT WAS THIRTY YEARS AGO, I REMEMBER THE day I met Xenia Lemos as if it was yesterday. My dear friend Franco Ammannati had heard that a vivacious young Greek woman had recently opened a beautiful *agriturismo* near Florence and was using our Cucina Fresca dinnerware for her guests. A blend of the Italian words *agricoltura* (agriculture) and *turismo* (tourism), an agriturismo is a working Italian farm that is designed to welcome guests to dine or stay. Agriturismi range from rustic to luxurious, and they are a wonderful and unique way to experience the natural beauty and bounty of Italy firsthand.

I desperately wanted to see our dinnerware in use, so I made a reservation to stay there and meet this woman. I drove through the rolling Chianti hills of Tuscany high above the city of Florence and found myself at a large

Once the doors swung open to invite me in, I was immediately transported into one of the most serene and idyllic environments I have ever been fortunate enough to enjoy.

wrought iron gate. Once the doors swung open to invite me in, I was immediately transported into one of the most serene and idyllic environments I have ever been fortunate enough to enjoy.

The path leading up to Xenia's agriturismo, named Casetta, is lined with tall, stately cypress trees. Hills of olive groves surround the property, and the gardens are lush, natural, and welcoming. At the end of the driveway sits the gorgeous,

Xenia and Susan sharing a cocktail and a laugh. Opposite page: Agriturismo Casetta.

119

270-year-old farmhouse, which has been in Xenia's family for generations. She had just finished the process of carefully restoring and revitalizing the property when I visited that first time, and I was completely enchanted by the spirit and aura of the place and its host.

Xenia welcomed me with what I now know to be her characteristic unflagging energy, authentic warmth, dry sense of humor, and genuine curiosity. She herself helped me with my luggage, walked me into the incredible home, and showed me to my room. I remember my bedroom's understated elegance, with its simple yet sumptuously soft linens, sophisticated yet comfortable furniture, and big, wide-open windows overlooking the gardens. I was one of her very first guests, but her natural hospitality and graciousness made it clear she was made for this role. She showed me through the grounds, and I marveled at the olive trees, the views of Tuscany, and the October sunset.

Next came dinner, and, as it was fall, I was treated to a fresh pasta with a creamy sauce of mushrooms straight from the garden. Xenia is famous for her homemade pasta dishes that feature savory sauces made with the best seasonal produce and local ingredients. I also remember homemade bread, a big green salad, and plenty of delicious Tuscan wine. Xenia and I took to each other right away at that dinner.

Born in Greece, educated in London, living in Tuscany, and fluent in three languages, Xenia had and has a unique perspective on the world, and I felt an instant kinship between us. We were two entrepreneurial women who cared deeply about creating beauty, we were fully transfixed by Italy, and we wanted to help people connect with one another over shared experiences, be it at the dinner table at home or on a trip to the Tuscan countryside. I remember feeling so inspired by this woman's brave path in life and by the fact that she could join us for a late, wine-filled dinner, be

A few vantage points of Casetta and some of its offerings: a lap pool, a setting al fresco, and an outdoor pizza oven.
Opposite page: A peek at Xenia's bar cabinet.

up before everyone else (working in the fields, no less), and then greet us later in the day with a big smile, a great story, and tempting suggestions for lunch!

Since that first stay, I have returned to Casetta as often as I am able. Bill and I have enjoyed leisurely days admiring Italy's scenery, resting, reading, and eating the freshest foods from Xenia's garden and favorite local bakeries and butcheries. I have stayed there with my sister and friends, lingering over long, family-style candlelit meals on Xenia's terrace, chatting about life, dreams, and shared memories. VIETRI even hosted a Board of Directors meeting at Casetta so that the

Board could soak up some Italian beauty. Xenia was present for one of our dinners, and a song that she loved came on over the sound system. She leapt up, I leapt up, and we began to dance. Before I knew it, everyone was up on their feet, shimmying and twirling and laughing under the night sky, Xenia's delight contagious.

My frequent visits to Casetta are in part because it is such a magnificent, world-class property—now with a glorious swimming pool, sculpture gardens, an outdoor brick oven for pizza-making parties, olive-harvesting classes, wine tastings, bike tours, truffle hunting, horseback riding, history tours, and more—but also because Xenia has become

The table set for lunch al fresco at Casetta.
Opposite page: The sitting room at Casetta.

one of my closest friends. Over the years, she has visited me in North Carolina, and we have become good friends with one another's friends and family. We have traveled together, gone to art shows together, and in 2021 she invited me on a girls' trip to Greece (I hadn't been on a girls' trip in decades). That trip was one of the best times in my recent memory. Never have I laughed so much, often to the point of tears and sore cheeks, all thanks to Xenia's unparalleled storytelling ability, impeccable comedic charm, and spot-on impressions. When one is with Xenia, one feels lit up by her zest for life and dynamism, and I think that is the reason Casetta has attracted visitors from America, Australia, Africa, and beyond. She exudes joy even when life is tough, and she is hardworking and unpretentious despite the fact that she has created such an oasis of luxury in the countryside. She looks for the good in others and is energized by connection and enjoying all that life has to offer. To be at Casetta is to take a deep breath, relax, and savor all that is wonderful about this world and its people.

I am delighted that Xenia is sharing a few of her favorite recipes with you here. I recommend Casetta to everyone I know, but until you can get there, I hope these give you a taste of its magic.

THE GUARNIERI BROTHERS

Bill and I spend two to three months in Florence each winter. We love walking around the city, exploring different areas, and marveling at the architecture.

One afternoon, we wandered into the lobby of a beautiful hotel called Hotel Regency. We decided to stop for a drink in the garden bar, and we were taken with the paintings displayed in the garden. We learned that they were done by a pair of local brothers named the Guarnieris or Iguarnieri (plural in Italian). We asked our waiter about the artists and left with their business card in hand. Soon after, we happened upon the Portrait Hotel on the Arno River, and all along the outside wall to the entrance were more Iguarnieri paintings. It seemed like a sign, so we decided that a Iguarnieri painting or two would be the perfect memento from our winter in Florence.

The following week, we walked to their art gallery on the Arno River, and that is when the love affair began! Roberto and Rodolfo Guarnieri are the co-founders of Art Gallery Studio Iguarnieri in Florence. Their contemporary paintings use fresco surfaces and traditional techniques with modern materials. Bill and I ended up choosing a large black and white fresco painting of the Duomo in Florence that hangs in our dining room and a colorful painting of wine glasses for our bar.

When VIETRI's Board of Directors stayed at Casetta, I asked Roberto and Rodolfo to bring some of their art and give a talk on inspiration. They brought many pieces, but Xenia fell for three long and narrow paintings of cypress trees in vibrant colors. They were perfect for the long wall at the top of her stairs and are reminiscent of the alley of cypress trees leading to her home.

After that evening, many of our Board members went to the gallery and purchased favorites for their own homes as memories of our wonderful time together.

Clockwise from top:
Susan at home in Chapel Hill
with her Iguarnieri painting
of the Duomo; The Guarnieri
brothers at work in their
studio and outside; Roberto
and Rodolfo Guarnieri.

CROSTINI AL CAVOLO NERO
Tuscan Kale Crostini

Tuscan kale (also called dinosaur kale) is sweeter and less bitter than curly leaf kale. If you can't find Tuscan or Lacinato kale, you may substitute a similar amount of collard greens or cabbage, chopped into bite-size pieces.

Yields 10 to 12

Bring a large pot of salted water to a boil over medium-high heat. Add the kale and boil for 4 to 5 minutes, until al dente. Drain in a colander and squeeze dry using paper towels.

Toast the pine nuts in a dry skillet over medium heat for 2 to 3 minutes, stirring occasionally to prevent scorching.

Combine the cooked kale, pine nuts, garlic, sugar, cheese, salt, pepper, and vinegar in a food processor and process until blended. Add the olive oil in a steady stream and pulse until the mixture is smooth. Taste and add salt and pepper as needed.

Preheat the broiler.

Slice the baguette and place the slices on a rimmed baking sheet. Brush one side of the crostini with olive oil. Broil less than 1 minute, until toasted. Flip, and brush the other side of the slices with oil and toast less than 1 minute.

Spread the puréed kale on the crostini and top, if desired, with cooked cannellini beans.

INGREDIENTS

1 bunch Tuscan, dinosaur, or Lacinato kale (about ⅓ pound), washed, and central stems removed

½ cup pine nuts

4 cloves garlic, peeled

½ teaspoon sugar

⅓ cup grated pecorino cheese

½ teaspoon salt, plus enough for kale boiling water

¼ teaspoon black pepper

1 tablespoon white wine vinegar

⅓ cup extra virgin olive oil, plus more for toasting bread

1 baguette

Optional garnish: cooked cannellini beans

PASTA AL SUGO DI NOCI
Pasta with Walnut Sauce

Tossing the sauce with a tube-shaped or corkscrew pasta ensures that its delectable flavors are suffused throughout the dish. Walnuts are harvested in the fall in Italy, so this traditional dish is usually enjoyed in fall and winter.

Serves 6 to 8

Tear the bread into pieces and place into the bowl of a food processor. Add the milk, walnuts, garlic, cheese, and olive oil, and pulse 2 to 3 minutes, until the mixture is finely minced and a thick sauce is achieved.

Bring a large pot of salted water to a boil. Cook the pasta according to package directions. Reserve ½ cup pasta cooking water to adjust the sauce's consistency. Drain the pasta in a colander.

Toss the pasta and the sauce together in the cooking pot. Add the reserved pasta cooking water a little at a time, as needed to slightly thin the sauce.

Season with salt and pepper, and stir to fully combine. Serve immediately.

INGREDIENTS

1 slice rustic bread, crust removed

⅔ cup milk

2 cups walnuts

5 cloves garlic, peeled

2 cups grated Parmigiano-Reggiano cheese

2 tablespoons extra virgin olive oil

1 pound dried pasta, such as strozzapreti, casarecce, cavatappi, or gemelli

1½ teaspoons salt, plus enough for the pasta pot

1 teaspoon black pepper

PASTA AL SUGO DI POMODORI SECCHI E MENTA
Pasta with Sun-Dried Tomato and Mint Sauce

So delicious, this pasta features a fresh, tangy sauce (the mint is the secret weapon) and can be enjoyed warm or cold.

Serves 6 to 8

Combine the tomatoes, mint, oil, vinegar, tomato paste, garlic, salt, pepper flakes, and sugar in a food processor and pulse 1 minute until smooth, scraping down the sides of the bowl as needed. Transfer the sauce to a large bowl.

Bring a large pot of salted water to a boil over medium-high heat and cook the pasta according to package directions.

While pasta is cooking, toast the pine nuts in a dry skillet over medium heat for 2 to 3 minutes, stirring occasionally to prevent scorching.

When the pasta is al dente, drain in a colander and reserve ½ cup of the pasta cooking water to adjust the sauce's consistency.

Add the pasta and the sauce back to the cooking pot. Add the reserved pasta cooking water a little at a time as needed to slightly thin the sauce. Stir to combine and sprinkle with pine nuts.

Serve hot, and pass the grated cheese around the table.

INGREDIENTS

1 cup oil-packed, sun-dried tomatoes

½ cup packed fresh mint leaves

½ cup extra virgin olive oil

5 teaspoons white wine vinegar

4 teaspoons tomato paste

2 cloves garlic, peeled

1 teaspoon salt, plus enough for the pasta water

½ teaspoon red pepper flakes

¼ teaspoon sugar

1 pound pasta, such as penne

½ cup pine nuts

Optional garnish: 1 cup grated pecorino cheese

PASTA AL SUGO DI ROSMARINO E PANCETTA
Pasta with Rosemary and Pancetta Sauce

Who knew Italians love bacon (pancetta) as much as we do? This is pure comfort food, and it is a quick and easy solution for a satisfying dinner using simple ingredients.

Serves 4 to 6

Melt 3 tablespoons butter in a large skillet over medium heat. Add the whole garlic cloves and cook until deep brown, about 5 minutes. Remove garlic cloves and add the rosemary. Stir once or twice and immediately add the pancetta. Cook 10 to 12 minutes, or until crisp. Drain off all but 2 tablespoons of the pancetta drippings. Remove from the heat and set the skillet with the cooked pancetta aside.

Bring a large pot of salted water to a boil over medium-high heat. Cook the pasta according to package directions, then drain in a colander and toss with the sauce in the skillet over medium-low heat. Add the remaining 1½ tablespoons butter and toss the pasta with the cheese until the butter has melted. Serve immediately.

INGREDIENTS

4½ tablespoons unsalted butter, divided

2 cloves garlic, peeled and gently crushed

2 teaspoons finely chopped fresh rosemary

10 slices (about ¾ pound) pancetta, or bacon, cut into 1-inch pieces

Salt for the pasta pot

1 pound penne pasta

1 cup grated Parmigiano-Reggiano cheese

POLLO CON OLIVE E PINOLI
Chicken with Olives and Pine Nuts

If you cannot find Taggiasche or Gaeta olives, you may substitute Kalamata or any brine-cured, pitted Italian olives for this recipe. This traditional Tuscan dish calls for using dark meat chicken. If you choose to use white meat with the dark (or white meat only), you will need to reduce the cooking time, as white meat cooks faster. Check the tenderness of the meat every 10 minutes during the final bake time.

Serves 4 to 5

Combine the chicken pieces, potatoes, olives, garlic, onion, tomatoes, pine nuts, thyme, bay leaves, rosemary, oregano, olive oil, salt, and pepper in a large baking dish. Stir to coat the meat and vegetables with the oil and seasonings, and set aside at room temperature for 30 minutes to marinate.

Preheat oven to 400 degrees F.

Place the baking dish in the oven and bake for 30 minutes. Add the wine, and stir to mix. Continue baking another 30 to 40 minutes until the chicken is very tender. Serve hot.

INGREDIENTS

1 pound chicken thighs and legs

3 russet potatoes, peeled and cut into large 2-inch chunks

1 cup pitted Taggiasche or Gaeta olives

4 cloves garlic, peeled

1 large onion, peeled and quartered

16 cherry tomatoes, halved

2 tablespoons pine nuts

4 sprigs thyme

4 bay leaves

1 sprig rosemary

1 tablespoon dried oregano

½ cup olive oil

1 teaspoon salt

½ teaspoon black pepper

1 cup dry white wine

PICCATA DI VITELLO
Veal Piccata

Rich and saucy, this has long been a favorite dish in Italy and America alike. The meat doesn't need to be tenderized as long as you make sure the veal cutlets are thin enough to cook quickly. You can press the cutlets with a broad knife if you need to make them thinner.

Serves 4 to 6

Cut one lemon in half lengthwise and slice one of the halves into ¼-inch thick rounds. Juice enough of the remaining lemons to obtain ¼ cup juice. Set aside.

Salt and pepper each cutlet generously. Place flour on a plate and dip each side of each cutlet in the flour to coat. Shake off excess and set the floured cutlets aside on a clean platter.

Preheat oven to 200 degrees F.

Heat 2 tablespoons oil in a large heavy-bottomed skillet over medium-high heat. Sauté half of the cutlets 2 to 4 minutes per side, until medium brown. Transfer the cutlets to an oven-safe platter and place in the warm oven. Add another 2 tablespoons oil, if needed, and cook the remaining cutlets. Keep all the cooked cutlets warm in the oven while you make the sauce.

Reduce the heat under the skillet to medium. Add the minced shallot and sauté 30 seconds until fragrant. Add the chicken stock and lemon slices, increase the heat to high and deglaze the pan, stirring to remove all the brown bits on the bottom. Simmer until the liquid reduces to about ⅓ cup. Add the lemon juice and capers and simmer until sauce again reduces to ⅓ cup.

Remove the pan from heat, stir in the butter until it melts and the sauce thickens. Stir in the parsley. Spoon the sauce over the cutlets and serve immediately.

INGREDIENTS

2 large lemons

Salt and pepper

1½ pounds veal scallopine or chicken or turkey cutlets

½ cup flour

¼ cup olive oil, divided

1 large shallot, peeled and minced

1 cup chicken stock

2 tablespoons capers, drained

3 tablespoons unsalted butter, at room temperature

2 tablespoons minced Italian parsley

CHAPTER 6

Kindred Spirits

FRANCES & ED MAYES, TUSCANY

FELLOW NORTH CAROLINIANS WHO ALSO FEEL AT HOME
in Italy, Frances and Ed Mayes are kindred spirits to me. Our paths first crossed
professionally with a commissioned dinnerware collection in honor of Frances's
bestselling book *Under the Tuscan Sun,* and that project was the start of a rich,
decades-long friendship. Momma, Frances, and I have had the joy of Frances and
Ed's company in their homes in Hillsborough, North Carolina, and in Cortona,
Italy, and no matter where we are geographically, we have always felt inspired,
welcomed, and at ease in their warm company.

Frances and Ed are passionate and skilled cooks whose enthusiasm for good
food is contagious. They are curious about culinary traditions, and they produce
their own delicious, award-winning olive oil from their olive groves in Cortona.
They also grow their own herbs, vegetables, and fruits so they can use the freshest
produce in their kitchen, following the Italian tenet that food tastes best when
it is simply prepared with high-quality ingredients. I have been lucky enough to
dine with them in their beautiful Italian home, Bramasole, many times, and I am
grateful to be the beneficiary of their gracious hospitality and culinary interests
and talents.

Bramasole is perched on a knoll above a winding road. It's an incredible,
250-year-old Italian farmhouse with terra cotta walls and light green shutters.

Susan with Frances Mayes
at Bramasole.
Opposite page: Bramasole, the
Cortona home of Frances and
Ed Mayes.

A descending, tiered garden unfolds in front of the house with flowering plants, stone walls, and walkways along which to amble. The home looks out on five acres of rolling green hills, cypress trees, and an expansive, brilliant sky. The Mayeses have kept the interior faithful to Italian tradition; the original walls are painted with soft, dreamy frescos, large stone fireplaces bring warmth and texture, exposed ceiling beams showcase the home's history and craftsmanship, ornate crystal chandeliers glimmer overhead, and rustic, wide-tiled floors are layered with beautiful rugs. The fabrics are both comfortable and rich, inviting one to sit down and stay a while.

A dinner party at Bramasole usually begins with enjoying a glass of prosecco or red wine in their open kitchen as they put the finishing touches on dinner.

While Bramasole is full of beautiful Italian antiques and has formal touches, it is Frances and Ed who inspire me by creating an inclusive, unpretentious, yet very special atmosphere for their guests. They have collected a diverse and rich group of friends over many years, and I always look forward to seeing who else might be invited to dinner—it could be the town librarian, a gardener, a dear family member, or a movie star!

A dinner party at Bramasole usually begins with enjoying a glass of prosecco or red wine in their open kitchen as they put the finishing touches on dinner. Including guests in the final stages of cooking has become one of my favorite ways to entertain as well; it puts everyone at ease and creates a familial, collaborative, and gracious atmosphere. There's no fluster or pressure to have a perfect final product before the doorbell rings; rather, it's a relaxed and easy way to start an evening. I remember when Frances and Ed told me that there was no Italian word for "stress" until Americans brought it over. Even though "stressato" now exists in the Italian vernacular, it is something I have never felt under their roof.

Before sitting down for dinner, Frances and Ed serve an inviting array of antipasti that showcases the bounty of the season. They have taught me how Italians roast chestnuts over the open fire during the holidays, and they've shared the way to make perfect bruschetta with fresh summer produce (the lesson remains to keep the recipe simple and use the best quality ingredients you can find). Next, the party moves to the dining room, where Frances loves to set creative, unexpected, and gorgeous tablescapes. Linen tablecloths and napkins dress the

Opposite page: The dining room at Bramasole.

table, and down the center are a collection of treasures from the house—small sculptures, little bowls, tall candles, and more. The effect is unique and artistic, and it has encouraged me to remember to look around my own house first when I'm putting together my table at home. The menu always features what is in season, served in traditional Italian style.

What strikes me the most about these dinners at Bramasole is the twinkly-eyed, curious, and youthful nature of the hosts. Conversations take the most fascinating turns because Frances and Ed are interested in everyone and everything. They are adept at finding common ground with anyone, yet they are always delighted to learn something new. Dinners at their house continue long after dessert is enjoyed, as everyone lingers at the table, sharing memories and adventures. The Mayeses have a way of making their guests feel appreciated and valued at their table, and that is something I endeavor to recreate for guests in my own home.

During a recent visit, Frances and I walked into a local art gallery in Cortona that had three prints of Bramasole on display. The owner of the gallery, a friend of Frances's, said that they always sell quickly thanks to Frances's bestselling book. Everyone wants to own a piece of that life under the Tuscan sun! I hope Frances's favorite recipes will give you a taste of that wonderful life.

Frances is a collector of all things Italian, from dinnerware to antique picture frames and religious icons.

20 YEARS AT BRAMASOLE

In honor of their 20th year at Bramasole, Frances and Ed hosted an incredible celebration in Cortona. I was unable to attend, but my sister was thrilled at the invitation. The evening began with a cocktail party in the lush gardens. Prosecco flowed, and waiters circulated with tremendously large rounds of Parmesan, slicing off pieces to pair with crackers for the guests. The five-course dinner took place at a beautiful hotel named Il Falconiere down the road, and the merry group sat at a 30-foot-long table under the stars. The candlelit table was adorned with hydrangeas and was narrow enough that you could easily talk with those across from you as well as by your side. The atmosphere was intimate and magical. My sister remembers all kinds of jubilant, joyous toasting, and that the evening, though at a lovely hotel with the most delicious of foods and most illustrious of guests, had a typical Italian easy elegance to it. The ambiance was laid-back yet luxurious, simple yet sophisticated. All felt welcome at the table and grateful to be together. It was just like Frances and Ed's life—joyous and special.

Frances and Ed share a toast on the evening of their al fresco dinner party. Opposite page: Bill and Susan share a toast with Frances and Ed at Bramasole.

CROSTINI DI PISELLI E SCALOGNO
Pea and Shallot Crostini

Crostini are toasted slices of a finely textured bread loaf, usually a baguette. Bruschetta is also toasted, but it uses larger slices of a rustic Italian or sourdough bread.

Yields 8 to 10

Heat the olive oil in a medium sauté pan over medium heat. Add the shallots and peas and sauté 4 minutes, or until the peas are barely done and the shallots are wilted. Stir in the mint, mascarpone, salt, and pepper.

Transfer to a food processor and coarsely chop.

Spoon onto the toasted bruschetta or crostini and serve at room temperature.

INGREDIENTS

2 tablespoons extra virgin olive oil

4 shallots, minced

2 cups fresh peas, shelled

3 tablespoons chopped mint

2 tablespoons mascarpone

¼ teaspoon salt

¼ teaspoon black pepper

8 to 10 slices bruschetta or crostini, toasted

CROSTINI DI SALAME, PECORINO, E NOCI
Salami, Pecorino, and Nut Crostini

This five-minute appetizer is a crowd-pleaser, and I can't imagine anything easier or better!

Yields 8

Place a slice of meat, cheese, and some walnuts on each piece of bread.

Place under broiler for a couple of minutes, until the cheese begins to melt. Serve warm or at room temperature.

INGREDIENTS

8 slices salami or prosciutto

8 slices pecorino or fontina cheese

¼ cup chopped walnuts

8 slices bruschetta or crostini

RISOTTO PRIMAVERA
Spring Risotto

Risotto is as versatile as pasta. Vary it by season, using roasted butternut squash in autumn and broccoli florets in winter. Shrimp risotto with lots of lemon juice and garlic is a summer staple at our house.

Serves 6

Season the peas with salt and pepper, and briefly steam them for 3 or 4 minutes in a covered saucepot over medium-high heat. The vegetables in this recipe should all remain crisp. Set aside.

Season the asparagus with salt and pepper, and break the asparagus stalks where they naturally snap. You can either steam them for 3 to 5 minutes, or roast them in a 375 degree F oven until barely done. Set aside.

If not slender, cut the carrots into pieces about the same size as the asparagus stems. Roast the carrots until barely done. Set aside.

Heat the chicken stock and wine in a large saucepan over high heat. Bring to a boil, then reduce the heat to medium-low to simmer while you begin the rice.

In another heavy 6-quart pot, heat the olive oil over medium heat. Add the rice and onion and sauté for 2 to 3 minutes, stirring to coat, until the rice browns. Stir in the salt and pepper.

Add one ladleful of stock and stir constantly as the rice absorbs the liquid. Keep stirring and ladling in more liquid for about 20 minutes, until the rice is done. Some prefer their risotto almost soupy, but for this dish it is better if the rice is moist and almost al dente. You may not use all the stock before the rice is done to your liking.

Remove the rice from heat and add the zest and lemon juice. Stir in the cheese, and season with more salt and pepper as needed.

Serve immediately in large shallow bowls with the vegetables surrounding a portion of rice.

INGREDIENTS

3 pounds fresh peas, shelled

2 bunches asparagus

1 bunch slender carrots, peeled

5½ cups chicken stock

½ cup white wine

1 tablespoon extra virgin olive oil

2 cups (1 pound) carnaroli or Arborio rice

1 yellow onion, finely chopped

1 teaspoon salt, plus more to taste

1 teaspoon black pepper, plus more to taste

Juice and zest of 1 lemon

½ cup grated Parmigiano-Reggiano cheese

INVOLTINI DI MELANZANE
Eggplant Rolls

In this creative and satisfying recipe, eggplant slices become the wrap for a delicious filling of meat and cheese. Be sure you slice the eggplant about ½-inch thick; if it's too thin or too thick it won't wrap easily. Also, use the brick-shaped part-skim mozzarella as it has less moisture. This is my all-time favorite dish!

Serves 8 to 10

Preheat the oven to 400 degrees F.

Line a baking sheet with parchment and oil the parchment. Place the eggplant slices on the pan and brush both sides with 2 tablespoons olive oil. Sprinkle with oregano, salt, and pepper. Bake for only 10 minutes, turning after 5 minutes.

While the eggplant is in the oven, make a simple tomato sauce by whirring tomatoes briefly in a food processor.

Sauté the onion for 2 to 3 minutes in the remaining 1 tablespoon olive oil in a medium skillet over medium heat. Add the garlic and sauté for 1 minute. Stir in the chopped tomatoes and cook for 2 minutes, just to blend the flavors.

Remove the eggplant from the oven.

Lower the oven temperature to 350 degrees F. Place a slice of prosciutto and a slice of mozzarella on each eggplant slice. Roll the pieces from the small end forward, and secure the little bundle with a toothpick or by tying a chive around it. Slather the bottom of a 9 x 13-inch baking dish with some of the tomato sauce and arrange the involtini seam side down. Over each bundle, spread some more sauce and a scattering of cheese.

Warm for 15 minutes in the oven and serve immediately.

INGREDIENTS

3 tablespoons extra virgin olive oil, divided, plus more for the parchment

1 large eggplant, cut lengthwise into 8 or 10 slices

1 tablespoon fresh oregano leaves, or 1½ teaspoons dried oregano

1 teaspoon salt

½ teaspoon black pepper

8 tomatoes, chopped, or 1 (28-ounce) can whole tomatoes, saving some of the liquid for the sauce

1 yellow onion, coarsely chopped

1 clove garlic, minced

8 slices prosciutto

8 slices mozzarella

¼ cup grated Parmigiano-Reggiano cheese

GELATO ALLA NOCCIOLA E LIMONE
Lemon Hazelnut Gelato

When you toast the hazelnuts for this recipe, watch them carefully as they can burn easily. After five minutes, wrap them in a dish towel, and rub off and discard the fine brown skins.

Serves 8 to 10 (about 2 quarts)

Beat the yolks and sugar in a medium bowl until well incorporated.

Heat the half-and-half in a medium saucepan over medium-high heat. Bring almost to a boil, then remove from the heat.

Whisk ½ cup of the heated half-and-half into the yolks and sugar mixture, and bring the saucepan to a good simmer over medium heat. Stir this back into the hot half-and-half saucepan. Bring the mixture back to a simmer, and stir constantly for 5 minutes, until the cream mixture thickens enough to coat a wooden spoon. Don't allow the pot to boil. If lumps form, strain through a fine mesh strainer.

Set the ice cream base aside in a bowl and whisk in the Frangelico, or vanilla, and heavy cream, and add the chopped hazelnuts and lemon zest.

Chill the mixture thoroughly, 7 to 8 hours. Stir well again and process as your ice cream machine requires.

INGREDIENTS

6 egg yolks

1½ cups sugar

1 quart half-and-half

1 tablespoon Frangelico (hazelnut liqueur), or 1 teaspoon vanilla extract

2 cups heavy cream

1½ cups hazelnuts, toasted and chopped

Zest of 1 lemon

FROLLINI AL PROFUMO DI ARANCIA E SALVIA
Orange and Sage Scented Shortbread Biscuits

Shortbread is a versatile and quick cookie to bake. It freezes well, too. You can make a simple version with a little vanilla, skipping the flavors below. Another delightful variation? Cut the shortbread into bars and dip them individually into chocolate.

Yields 2 dozen

Combine the butter and sugar in a medium bowl and beat until fluffy. Add the flour, salt, zest, and sage leaves, and mix until the dough comes together.

Divide the dough into two equal portions and roll out 2 (2½ to 3-inch diameter) logs on a lightly-floured surface. Wrap with plastic wrap, and chill the dough for at least two hours.

Preheat the oven to 325 degrees F.

Cut the cookies into ½-inch slices and place on a parchment-lined baking sheet. Bake for 25 minutes. Check after 20 minutes for doneness; cookies should be slightly firm to the touch.

Remove with a spatula to a wire cooling rack and serve warm, or at room temperature.

INGREDIENTS

8 ounces unsalted butter, softened

½ cup sugar

2 cups all-purpose flour, sifted

Pinch of salt

1 tablespoon orange zest

6 fresh sage leaves, minced

CHAPTER 7

Venetian Vigor
THE VENZO FAMILY, VENETO

I MET MARIANO VENZO IN MILAN IN 1985 AT THE MACEF
International Gift Show. I came across his booth, and I was taken by his designs'
nuanced textures, creative shapes, and artistic painting. I immediately decided I
needed to see more, so I made the three-hour trip to Nove in the Veneto region of
Italy to see his factory. There, I marveled at the skill of the artisans, the sophistication
of the designs, and the impeccable Italian quality of everything they produced.

I was taken by his designs'
nuanced textures, creative
shapes, and artistic painting.

Mariano and I soon began designing something special for
VIETRI, and our first collection together was called Tulipani
d'Acqua or Water Tulips. Frances and I presented the collection
at the January New York Gift Show in 1989, and the tabletop
buyer for Neiman Marcus, Greg Smith, was particularly struck
by it. Neiman Marcus ended up buying it in droves, and it fortunately turned out
to be a hugely successful collection for them. To celebrate the collection's triumph,
Neiman Marcus invited us to a beautiful dinner in New York. Mariano was invited
as well, and so he eagerly got on a plane and flew to America for a wonderful
evening. Greg, Frances, Momma, Mariano, and I went to Ristorante Lupa, where
we made merry with lots of wine, filet mignon, and good spirits. Neiman Marcus
had ordered a limousine for us, and after our dinner we took a tour around the

Susan and Mariano Venzo.
Opposite page: The Venzos'
home in Nove, Italy.

city, seeing the sights and lights. I recently asked Mariano what he remembers of that special night, and his main memories are of Momma and how enchanted he was by her poise, elegance, and warmth.

During the ensuing years, I visited Mariano a few times a year. Our friendship and professional relationship deepened with each visit, and I soon began receiving invitations to join his family for dinner in their home. This was a big honor, and I remember that first meal back in 1996 as if it was yesterday. The gathering was warm and welcoming, with Mariano's wonderful wife, Agnese, and three children present, and we ate in

the Venzos' big kitchen that has a beautiful terrace off to the side. We started with an assortment of antipasti featuring the region's freshest vegetables, cheeses, and meats, and then Mariano fired up the wood-burning grill to cook a feast of lamb, beef, and chicken. He is a true grill master, and his biggest tips are to keep the grill HOT and salt the meat after cooking it. He served the grilled meats with fried potatoes, grilled radicchio, and generous amounts of red wine. A delicious dessert was brought in from the nearby *pasticceria*.

Seasonal vegetables and Incanto Dinnerware in the Venzos' kitchen.
Opposite page: Agnese, Mariano, Susan, and Bill enjoying a toast.

Agnese had spent the day preparing for the meal. As I got to know her better and joined in for more of these family meals, I noticed the amount of attention, time, and care she put into preparing for each of these gatherings. They are a true labor of love for her, as she would start setting the table around 2 p.m. with plates and linens in colors that matched the season. The table's decoration also reflected the time of year, with fresh flowers in the spring or rich leaves in the fall. She placed tall candles throughout the room, and the effect was inviting and intimate. When I join the Venzos for meals now, there is a new generation present, as Mariano and Agnese's three children have all married (I was very honored to attend each of their weddings) and have children of their own. I love how the youthful presence keeps everything relaxed and joyful.

> *Mariano and I have had a number of adventures that, while nerve—racking at the time, now bring us great laugher in recollection.*

Speaking of joy, Mariano and I have had a number of adventures that, while nerve-racking at the time, now bring us great laughter in recollection. In VIETRI's early days, we decided to do a photoshoot with Mariano's designs while we were in Italy. There is a famous wooden bridge in Bassano del Grappa called Ponte degli Alpini. Designed in 1569, it is steeped in history. It has been destroyed in times of war and rebuilt in times of peace. Frances and I thought it would be the perfect Italian backdrop for our dinnerware collections, so we unpacked our products, displayed them artfully, and had a photographer start snapping pictures. Little did we know that taking commercial photos on this national monument was illegal, but we quickly got the gist when we saw angry policemen walking in our direction, ready to scold us. Despite being Italian, the photographer quickly pretended not to understand the policemen's language, and Mariano, the one who was supposed to be our guide in this town, ran and hid, no help to us at all! This left Frances and me stammering fuzzy explanations and excuses in Italian in order to fend off the policemen just long enough for our photographer to snap the last remaining shots we needed of the products on the bridge.

Lest you think Mariano always fears authority, that was not the case one night in North Carolina. To honor the North Carolina Museum of Art's 50th anniversary in 1997, VIETRI was commissioned to create a charger featuring the designs of seven major pieces of art found in the museum. La Ceramica VBC, Mariano's factory,

Opposite page: The Ponte degli Alpini in Bassano del Grappa.

produced this piece for the museum. Mariano and his nephew, Carlo, attended the anniversary gala along with Bill and me. The evening was a lovely celebration, and I had offered to be the designated driver on the way home. We were driving through my neighborhood when I, a bit irresponsibly, slowly rolled through a stop sign to turn onto my street. Policemen were lying in wait, and they immediately turned on their flashing lights and sirens. I pulled over, and before I knew what was happening, Mariano, in typical Italian fashion, leapt out of the car to defend my honor. This is customary in Italy, but I started yelling at him, "Mariano! GET BACK IN THE CAR! We don't do that here!" as I also tried to explain the cultural difference to the American policemen! Fortunately, all's well that ends well, and Mariano has yet to add seeing the inside of an American jail to his list of travel experiences. We are grateful to have escaped both of our brushes with the law!

Mariano and Bill have become great friends and enjoy hiking and fishing together (which sounds much more peaceful and pleasant than my rule-breaking escapades with Mariano). Our families have all become close, and I hope that a peek into the Venzos' kitchen and a taste of the wonderful recipes they have shared bring you the same delight and joy that they have brought me.

Lunch at the Venzos' home.
Opposite page: The nearby town of Marostica where Mariano loves to visit his favorite cheese shop, Famiglia Gastaldello dal 1969.

Clockwise from top: Susan receives a framed set of keys at La Festa della Ceramica; Susan and the Mayor of Nove; The town of Nove prepares for the celebration; The town streets filled with tables for the banquet.

THE KEYS TO NOVE

I received a frantic call one day from Mariano during the summer of 2002. He excitedly told me that I would be receiving the keys to the town of Nove on Saturday, September 14. I had to ask him to repeat himself, as I was having difficulty understanding his rather breathless enthusiasm. Sure enough, what I had heard was correct. I would be named an honorary citizen of Nove for the work and energy I had brought to their ceramic town. *Wow.* I was so flattered!

A few days before flying out, I casually told Bill about this honor. I imagined I would go to City Hall, and they would hand me a sheet of paper at a small ceremony. Bill immediately called my mother, and they each purchased plane tickets so they could join me—under no circumstances would this event take place without their presence.

When Momma, Bill, and I arrived in Nove on the day before the event, there were banners in the town piazza proudly advertising La Festa della Ceramica. We saw tables and chairs being set up along the main street. There was an enormous bandstand with tents, and banners and flags were hoisted throughout the city. This was really going to be something!

Saturday finally arrived. We started the evening with drinks at Mariano's house. We toasted with prosecco, and off we went to the piazza. We arrived to find the *sindaco* (mayor), other dignitaries, and numerous leaders of other factories. There were colorful banners flying and music and gaiety and about 200 people lined up along the road, all coming to congratulate me. Soon arrived the town's majorettes and marching band. We had a lovely four-course dinner, followed by a quartet and opera singers from Milan's La Scala. I could hardly believe it was all for me.

The town's mayor began with a speech to welcome everyone there, and then he turned to me. He shared that I had brought great pride, great creativity, and great economic benefits to their town. VIETRI was known all over Italy, and they were proud to be a part of it. I was invited forward and handed framed keys, a framed honorarium with a silk ribbon, and a large ceramic whistle made out of clay, molded like Napoleon on a horse. It seems that when Napoleon came through the Veneto region, known for ceramics, all of the people blew small ceramic hand whistles to warn that the French were arriving.

After the presentation, I thanked everyone in my best Italian, and I hope that I was able to convey just how deeply grateful I was. I was thrilled to share the night with Momma and Bill. It was truly special. When the four-hour dinner and ceremony concluded, I looked at Momma and Bill and laughed, "I had no idea! Thank you so much for coming. I would have been so sad to do this alone!"

Over the years, I have been honored to receive keys to two more cities in Italy, but I will never forget that first time and what it meant to me.

ZUPPA DI FUNGHI MISTI
Mixed Mushroom Soup

Italian 00 flour, also known as doppio zero, is a super-fine flour used for making pasta and pizza dough. It can be found at most grocery stores, Italian specialty markets, or online. If you can't find oyster or portobello mushrooms, you may substitute either shiitake or enoki for a similar version of this rich, creamy soup. This is a mushroom-lovers must!

Serves 4

Bring 8 cups water to a boil in a teapot.

Melt the butter in a Dutch oven or soup pot over medium heat. Add the onion and sauté 3 to 5 minutes until translucent and lightly browned. Add the garlic and continue sautéing 2 more minutes. Increase the heat to high, and add the mushrooms. Cook for 15 to 20 minutes, stirring occasionally.

When the mushrooms are cooked and no longer releasing any liquid, reduce the heat to medium, add the flour, and stir. Slowly add the boiling water, stirring constantly until well combined and no lumps of flour remain. Season with salt and pepper to taste.

Reduce the heat to medium-low and cook for another 20 minutes, stirring occasionally. Add the cream and chopped parsley, if using, incorporating them well.

Season with salt and pepper as needed.

INGREDIENTS

4 tablespoons unsalted butter

½ cup finely chopped onion

1 clove garlic, minced

18 ounces mixed mushrooms, such as portobello and oyster, cleaned and coarsely chopped

3 tablespoons Italian 00 flour

1 teaspoon salt, plus more to taste

½ teaspoon black pepper, plus more to taste

¼ cup heavy cream

Optional garnish: chopped Italian parsley

POLENTA

One of the oldest dishes in Italy, polenta is currently most popular in the Veneto region, and it shows up regularly on family and restaurant tables at lunch and dinner. It is cooked on top of the oven to a consistency that reminds me of our Southern grits. It can be eaten warm in a bowl at this stage, but this recipe calls for it to be cooled and cut into squares.

Serves 4 to 6

Place 6 cups water, oil, and salt in a medium saucepan over high heat and bring to a boil. When it boils, sprinkle the polenta into the boiling water. Whisk vigorously 1 to 2 minutes to prevent lumps.

Lower the heat to medium and cook 40 minutes, stirring frequently. If polenta gets too thick to stir with a whisk, switch to a wooden spoon. Polenta is done when each grain is tender and the mixture is creamy. Remove from heat.

Pour the polenta into an oiled 8 x 8-inch baking dish and let it sit at room temperature until it reaches a semi-firm consistency. Slice into squares and top with softened butter and the Parmigiano-Reggiano cheese as desired.

INGREDIENTS

3 tablespoons olive oil

1 teaspoon salt

1 cup polenta

Optional garnish:
2 tablespoons butter,
½ cup grated
Parmigiano-Reggiano
cheese

PATATE ARROSTO
Roasted Potatoes

Roasted potatoes seem to be a beloved side dish in almost any country, and this recipe is a great way to ensure they are always tender and delicious. If you increase the cooking temperature during the last 5 minutes, the potato skin will be even more crispy.

Serves 4 to 6

Preheat the oven to 350 degrees F.

Fill a medium saucepan ⅔ full of water. Add 1 teaspoon salt to water and bring to a boil over medium heat.

When water comes to a boil, add the potatoes and cook for 1 minute. Drain the potatoes in a colander.

Place the potatoes on a rimmed baking sheet and sprinkle with oil, the remaining 1 teaspoon salt, and pepper. Stir to coat and bake for 20 minutes, until lightly browned. Remove from the oven and stir in the rosemary, sage, and garlic to fully coat. Reduce the oven temperature to 320 degrees F and cook for another 12 to 15 minutes, until they reach the desired tenderness.

Remove from the oven, stir gently, and serve hot.

INGREDIENTS

2 teaspoons salt, divided

2 pounds Yukon Gold potatoes, peeled and cut into 1-inch cubes

¼ cup olive oil

¼ teaspoon black pepper

1 tablespoon minced fresh rosemary

1 tablespoon minced fresh sage

1 clove garlic, minced

RISOTTO AL RADICCHIO ROSSO
Risotto with Red Radicchio

Italian Vialone Nano is a medium-grain rice grown in the southern province of Verona, in the Veneto region. It can be purchased online or at Italian specialty markets. If you cannot find it, you may substitute Arborio rice.

Serves 8

Bring the broth to a simmer in a saucepan over low heat.

Heat 2 tablespoons butter and olive oil in a large skillet over medium heat. Sauté the onion and garlic for 3 to 5 minutes until the onions are translucent. Add the radicchio, salt, and pepper and cook 2 to 3 minutes, stirring constantly with a wooden spoon. Stir in the red wine, which helps enhance the red of the risotto. Remove the garlic and carefully stir in 1½ teaspoons sugar and the rice. Reduce the heat to medium-low.

Add one cup broth to the rice, stirring constantly with a wooden spoon until the broth is almost absorbed, then add the next cup of broth and repeat the process, stirring often, until all the broth is absorbed and the rice is fully cooked and tender. This process can take up to 45-60 minutes.

When the rice is almost ready, taste and add the remaining 1½ teaspoons sugar and more salt and pepper as needed. Whisk in the remaining 2 tablespoons butter and cheese.

Serve rice hot and pass with more cheese if desired.

INGREDIENTS

8 cups chicken broth

4 tablespoons unsalted butter, divided

¼ cup extra virgin olive oil

1 medium red onion, finely chopped

1 clove garlic, whole

2 heads radicchio, washed and cut into bite-sized pieces

1 teaspoon salt, plus more to taste

¼ teaspoon black pepper, plus more to taste

½ cup red wine

3 teaspoons sugar, divided

1½ cups Vialone Nano, or Arborio rice

1 cup grated Parmigiano-Reggiano cheese

POLLO ALLA CACCIATORA
Chicken Cacciatore

Chicken Cacciatore has several variations; this one is the simplest. Feel free to add chopped green peppers, sliced mushrooms, peas, capers, or olives along with the tomatoes. Enjoy it with polenta (recipe, see page 176) or potato purée on the side.

Serves 6 to 8

Heat the olive oil and butter in a Dutch oven or large lidded skillet over medium heat. Brown the chicken pieces in the hot oil, about 3 to 4 minutes per side.

Once browned, add the onion and sauté for 3 to 5 minutes until the onions are translucent. Add the tomatoes, salt, and pepper, reduce the heat to low, cover, and cook for 30 minutes, or until the internal temperature of the chicken reaches 165 degrees F.

Use a slotted spatula to remove the chicken to a platter.

Add the wine to the sauce in the pan. Increase the heat to medium and cook 8 to 10 minutes, stirring occasionally, until the sauce reduces and thickens.

Spoon sauce into individual bowls, or onto a serving platter, and top with the chicken pieces.

INGREDIENTS

2 tablespoons olive oil

2 tablespoons unsalted butter

1 whole chicken, cut up in pieces, or 4 chicken thighs and 2 bone-in chicken breasts, cut in half

1 medium onion, diced

1 (28-ounce) can diced tomatoes

2 teaspoons salt

1 teaspoon black pepper

½ cup dry white wine

TARASSACO IN PADELLA
Pan-Fried Dandelion

If you forage dandelion, it must be picked in the countryside during the spring, far from busy roads, and in fields without chemical treatment. Luckily, it is also available seasonally at some grocery stores and farmers markets.

Serves 6 to 8

Trim the bottom ends of the dandelion.

Place 6 cups water and the salt in a medium pot over high heat and bring to a boil. Add the dandelion, lower the heat to medium-high, and cook for 8 to 10 minutes until the ribs are tender.

Drain in a colander and set aside. Then, use paper towels to squeeze out as much water as possible from the dandelion greens. Place on a cutting board and chop into bite-sized pieces.

Heat the oil in a large skillet over medium heat. Add the bacon and cook for 5 to 8 minutes until crisp. Add the minced garlic and cook for 1 minute, then reduce the heat to low. Add the dandelion and cook for 10 minutes, stirring constantly. Add the vinegar, pepper, and salt to taste, and serve immediately.

INGREDIENTS

2¼ pounds dandelion, roots cleaned and outermost leaves removed

1 tablespoon salt, plus more to taste

2 tablespoons extra virgin olive oil

3 slices bacon, minced

3 cloves garlic, minced

1 tablespoon white wine vinegar

¼ teaspoon black pepper

TORTA DI MELE CLASSICO
Classic Apple Cake

Many Italians prefer fruit desserts to chocolate ones, and apple recipes are a particular favorite. This recipe is very adaptable, however, so feel free to substitute with whatever fruit is in season, such as pears, figs or peaches.

Serves 8 to 10

Preheat the oven to 350 degrees F.

Line the bottom of a springform pan with parchment paper. Butter the bottom and sides of the pan and set aside.

Toss the slices of 1 apple with ¼ cup sugar, the lemon juice, and zest.

Whisk the eggs with ¼ cup sugar in a medium bowl. Stir in the olive oil and melted butter. Fold in the flour, baking powder, salt, and ¼ cup milk until thoroughly combined.

Gently fold in half of the remaining slices and their juice. The batter will be stiff. Evenly spread over the bottom of pan.

Arrange the remaining apple slices in a radial pattern on the top of the batter and sprinkle with the remaining ¼ cup sugar.

Bake for 25 minutes. Lower the heat to 300 degrees F and bake for another 20 to 30 minutes, until an inserted toothpick comes out clean. Allow to cool slightly before serving.

INGREDIENTS

2 large baking apples, divided, peeled, cored, and cut into thin slices, juice reserved

¾ cup sugar, divided

Zest and juice of 1 lemon

2 eggs

2 tablespoons olive oil

5 tablespoons unsalted butter, melted

1¾ cups all-purpose flour

2 teaspoons bustina di lievito per dolci, or 1 teaspoon baking powder with a pinch of vanilla powder

Pinch of salt

¼ cup milk

LA CERAMICA VBC

Steeped in ceramic tradition, Nove has been a cradle of Italian design and innovation for more than 300 years. It is known throughout the world as the "City of Ceramics," and it is home to my dear friend Mariano and his wonderful factory, La Ceramica VBC. I feel as though Mariano and I have grown up together, as we met each other early in our careers and have enjoyed an incredible entrepreneurial journey together since then.

Mariano founded VBC with his friends Leonardo and Paolo when they were all just 20 years old. Their parents had been ceramicists, and they had grown up in Nove, so the craft was in their blood. Mariano's brother Giovanni was the first maestro for VBC, and Mariano and Giovanni loved dreaming up fresh, original designs for the area's native soft, rich clays. Giovanni was the creative force for many years until his son, Francesco, took over. Francesco still leads the factory's designs today.

I love that VBC's designs honor Italy, perhaps best exemplified in our incredibly popular Incanto collection. Each motif from the collection represents a different and beautiful aspect of the region's history, geography, and culture: The ruffles paying homage to the waves of the Adriatic Sea, the pleated patterns mimicking the Teatro la Fenice, the stripes honoring stately Palladian columns, the lace nodding to Venice's Burano Island, and the curving swirls representing Baroque architecture. Francesco is truly masterful at transforming clay into works of art for the table. He creates Incanto in its original black, volcanic earthenware clay as well as a newer, chip-resistant stoneware.

VBC's designs have also been inspired by nature. On one of Mariano's visits to North Carolina, he and Bill gathered oak leaves during a hike. When Mariano returned home, he and Francesco dreamed up a collection featuring molds of these oak leaves as well as olive leaves from their region. Vibrant and unique, we decided to call the collection Foglia, meaning leaf in Italian, and it is a favorite collection that I use often in my own home!

Clockwise from top: Susan with Mariano, 1988; Paintbrushes at La Ceramica VBC; Maestro artisan Francesco Venzo molds a serving bowl from VIETRI's Incanto Dinnerware collection; Pieces from the Incanto Dinnerware collection.

The team at La Ceramica VBC with Susan and Bill.

CHAPTER 8

A Chance Encounter

THE FABBRO FAMILY, FRIULI-VENEZIA GIULIA

WHILE I HAVEN'T KNOWN HIM FOR AS LONG AS THE others in this book, Gianluca Fabbro has quickly become a wonderful friend and business partner. A fifth-generation artisan, Gianluca was presenting his designs at a market I attended in Frankfurt in 2015. Despite being weary from many long days of design scouting, I felt a jolt of energy and excitement the moment I first saw his original, innovative display. His collections were unlike anything I had ever seen before in all my years of ceramic research, and I immediately knew I wanted to add his creations to the VIETRI assortment. While sponging is common in ceramics, Gianluca's unique style of sponging has an unmatched level of detail, dimension, and vibrancy, and his talent and precision make every piece sing. What makes Gianluca even more of a sensation is that his incredible talent is matched only by his buoyant personality. He is joyous, creative, enthusiastic. I truly can't recall a time he has ever said "no," and I so admire his zest for life and living well.

I felt a jolt of energy and excitement the moment I first saw his original, innovative display.

Gianluca and his family live in Friuli-Venezia Giulia, a beautiful region of

Susan with Gianluca Fabbro. Opposite page: VIETRI's Limoni Dinnerware collection, handsponged by Gianluca.

Italy that borders Austria, Slovenia, and the Adriatic Sea. In my many visits to Gianluca's artisan workshop, I have had the pleasure of sampling the region's best and most famous culinary offerings. Due to its geographic location, the region's cuisine is an eclectic combination of Mediterranean flavors and rustic mountain dishes influenced by the countries to its north and east. The dishes tend to be hearty and meat-based, with rich cheeses and fresh seafood from the Adriatic. We have dined together in Friuli's mountain towns and seaside villages, and while the fare has varied due to the location, one thing always remains the same: We pause amidst our hectic schedules to sit down and enjoy a meal. No matter the demands of the day, taking a break is important to Gianluca (and to Italians in general), and it is felt that the rest of life can be better approached when one has had an hour or two to rest, eat a good meal, breathe, and relax. I know firsthand how challenging it is to adopt this mentality back home, but every time I travel to Italy and follow these habits and rituals for my stay, I am convinced that Italians have got it figured out.

The first time I was invited to eat with Gianluca and his family at their home,

The Fabbro home in Friuli-Venezia Giulia.
Opposite page, clockwise from top: The Fabbro Kitchen; VIETRI Fauna Dinnerware; VIETRI Pumpkins Dinnerware; Davide, Gianluca and Cristina's eldest son.

we ate in their beautiful dining room. The home is close to his factory, and it is U-shaped with a lovely garden courtyard. The dining room is paneled in rich, warm wood, and a large wooden table sits in the center. I first visited during wintertime, and the feeling was cozy and intimate. There was an ambiance of comfort and togetherness, and I remember laughter over candlelight, getting to know his wonderful wife, Cristina, and meeting his sons, Davide and Alberto. While northern Italy is more formal, there was nothing stuffy about the meal—just friends and family coming together after a day of work and school to enjoy good food and one another's company.

There was nothing stuffy about the meal— just friends and family coming together after a day of work and school to enjoy good food and one another's company.

Gianluca's eldest son, Davide, is tall and handsome. He has a wonderful tilt of the head and a twinkle in his eye, and he hopes to take over the design side of his family's business someday. I once asked him where he finds his artistic inspiration, and he said with a smile, "It's my father. He is my inspiration, especially in new designs." When I later told Gianluca what his son had said, Gianluca became teary and incredulously said, "No, no. I don't believe that; all Davide does is argue with me!" I told him it was indeed true. We laughed together about the loving and playful dynamics between parents and children. Gianluca told me he would cherish his son's tribute forever.

I recently had the pleasure of spending a month with Gianluca's youngest son, Alberto. Alberto is very interested in learning more about business, and so I invited him to come stay with us in North Carolina and intern at VIETRI.

Alberto arrived in July. He spent time in all our departments—HR, product development, marketing and sales, customer service, finance, product procurement, and warehousing. Though just a teenager, he generously offered

Alberto, Gianluca and Cristina's youngest son.

Bill and Susan share a toast with Gianluca and Cristina.

to cook for Bill and me one evening. The meal was so delicious that we eagerly asked him to prepare it again for a dinner party we were hosting later that week. He gamely said yes, and it was even better on night two!

The Fabbros are avid outdoorsmen, and their favorite recipes highlight the best of their region's game and produce. I have tried many new dishes thanks to Gianluca's suggestions, and I hope you will give some of his favorites a try in your own kitchen. You won't be disappointed!

FRITTATA ALLE ERBE
Herb Frittata

The basic difference between an omelet and a frittata is the latter is cooked slowly over low heat—sometimes even baked in the oven—while an omelet is cooked quickly over a medium or medium-high heat. Omelets are usually served immediately so they retain their heat, while frittatas are often served at room temperature. This is a great dish to make ahead for brunch.

Serves 8

Place the potatoes in a small pot and cover with water. Bring to a boil over medium-high heat and cook for 10 minutes until fork tender. Drain and set aside to cool.

In a medium bowl, beat the eggs with a fork. Add the chopped herbs, cheese, onion, salt, and pepper and stir to combine.

Cut the cooled potatoes into 1-inch chunks. Add to eggs and stir gently to combine.

Heat the oil in a large skillet over medium heat, making sure there is enough oil to just cover the entire bottom of the pan. Add the egg mixture and cook 4 to 5 minutes until the frittata thickens. Use a spatula to loosen around the edge. If you are good at flipping frittatas, turn the frittata over onto the other side and let cook for another 3 to 4 minutes until set. If not, you can finish using the oven broiler, cooking 3 to 4 minutes until the eggs are set.

Place the frittata on a serving plate or wooden cutting board, and cut into wedges. Garnish the center with a bunch of herbs and seasonal flowers.

INGREDIENTS

4 small red potatoes

10 eggs

1¼ cups mixed finely chopped herbs, such as dandelion, thyme, basil, oregano, or Italian parsley, plus some for garnish

¼ cup grated Montasio or Parmigiano-Reggiano cheese

¼ cup finely chopped onion

½ teaspoon salt

¼ teaspoon black pepper

¼ cup olive oil, or more as needed to cover the bottom of the pan

Optional garnish: seasonal edible flowers

ORZOTTO CON CREMA DI TARASSACO E PATATE
Pearl Barley with Dandelion and Potato Cream

This combination of creamy potato purée with barley and cooked vegetables makes a lovely side dish, but is hearty enough to be enjoyed as a meal in itself.

Serves 4

Preheat the oven to 350 degrees F.

Place the bacon slices on a parchment paper-lined rimmed baking sheet and bake for 30 to 35 minutes, until desired crispiness. Transfer to paper towels to drain.

Combine 3 cups water, the barley, carrots, celery, and onion in a medium saucepan. Bring to a simmer over medium heat and cook for 30 to 35 minutes until the barley is softened but still chewy. Drain and set aside.

While the bacon and barley are cooking, fill a large saucepan half full of water and bring to a boil over medium-high heat. Blanch the spinach or dandelion for 1 minute. Drain and squeeze with paper towels to remove excess water. Chop the greens on a cutting board and set aside.

Place the potatoes in a medium saucepan with enough water to cover, and bring to a boil over high heat. Cook for 5 to 8 minutes, until the potatoes are easily pierced with a knife. Drain.

Place the hot potatoes and butter in the bowl of a food processor. When the butter melts, add the milk, salt, and pepper, and purée until smooth.

Heat the oil in a skillet over medium heat. Add the barley mixture and the chopped greens and cook for 3 to 5 minutes until heated through.

Crumble the bacon. Divide the potato purée among four bowls. Top with a scoop of the barley/greens and sprinkle with the crispy bacon. Serve warm.

INGREDIENTS

4 slices bacon

3 cups water

1 cup pearl barley, or pearl farro

¼ cup diced carrots

¼ cup diced celery

¼ cup diced onion

1 bunch spinach or dandelion, washed and ends trimmed

1 large or 2 medium Yukon Gold potatoes, peeled and quartered

2 tablespoons butter, cubed, at room temperature

¼ cup warm milk

1 teaspoon salt

¼ teaspoon black pepper

2 tablespoons olive oil

INSALATA DI PETTO D'ANATRA CON CIALDE DI FRICO
Duck Breast Salad with Frico Wafers

These Frico wafers are so delicious that you'll want to make more of them to serve with appetizers and other dishes as well. Here, the peppery bites are a good pairing with the sweet balsamic glaze of the duck. This is a rich, satisfying salad for a winter lunch or evening meal.

Serves 4

Preheat oven to 400 degrees F.

In a small bowl, mix together the cheese, cayenne pepper, and black pepper.

On a silicone or parchment-lined rimmed baking sheet (a silicone baking sheet is highly recommended), arrange rounded tablespoonsful of the cheese mixture about 1 inch apart. Bake 3 to 5 minutes, until golden brown and crisp. Cool, then remove with a thin spatula and set aside.

Lower the oven temperature to 350 degrees F.

Season the duck with salt and pepper and place the breasts skin-side-down in a cold skillet. Cook on medium heat for 12 to 14 minutes, checking often to make sure the duck is not burning. Flip the duck breasts to meat-side-down and cook for 1 to 2 minutes, then transfer to a rimmed baking sheet, and place them skin-side-up.

Bake for 5 to 8 minutes. Remove and set aside to rest for 5 minutes.

Boil the eggs and chill in an ice bath for 15 minutes.

While the duck is cooking, make the balsamic glaze salad dressing. Heat the balsamic vinegar and sugar in a small saucepan over high heat. Once sauce comes to a simmer, reduce the heat to low and cook for 15 minutes, until the glaze reduces to a consistency thick enough to coat the back of a spoon. Set aside to cool slightly.

To complete the dressing, combine the balsamic glaze, the olive oil, ¼ teaspoon salt, and a few grinds black pepper in a small bowl. Whisk to fully combine.

To serve, divide the frico wafers among four plates and top each with 1 cup lettuce greens. Peel the eggs, cut into quarters, and arrange atop the lettuce. Slice the duck breasts and arrange atop each salad. Drizzle the balsamic dressing on each salad and serve immediately.

INGREDIENTS

Frico Wafers:

1 cup grated Montasio or Parmigiano-Reggiano cheese

Pinch of cayenne pepper

Two or three grinds of black pepper

Duck:

2 duck breasts

Salt and pepper, to taste

Salad:

4 boiled eggs, cut in quarters

½ cup balsamic vinegar

1½ teaspoons sugar

½ cup extra virgin olive oil

¼ teaspoon sea salt

Freshly ground pepper, to taste

4 cups salad greens, such as frisée, endive, or radicchio

COSCE DI CONIGLIO CON PATATE FRITTE
Rabbit Legs with Pan-Fried Potatoes

Rabbit is enjoyed throughout Italy, especially in the regions where hunting is a favorite sport. If you want to crisp the skin at the end of cooking, place the skillet into the oven at 425 degrees F for 5 minutes.

Serves 4

Heat 2 tablespoons olive oil in a large Dutch oven over medium-low heat.

Sauté the carrots, celery, and onion for 6 to 8 minutes, until the onions soften and begin to brown. Add 1 tablespoon oil to the onion mixture, and arrange the rabbit legs in a layer on the bottom of the pan. Brown the legs on one side, about 3 to 4 minutes, then turn them and brown the other side 3 or 4 minutes.

Add the white wine and use a spatula to loosen any brown bits on the bottom of the pan. Add the herbs, ½ teaspoon salt, and ¼ teaspoon pepper. Lower the heat a little, cover with lid and cook for 30 minutes.

While the rabbit cooks, heat the remaining 3 tablespoons olive oil in a large skillet over medium heat. Add the shallots, garlic, and chopped bacon, and sauté for 3 to 4 minutes. Add the potatoes, the remaining ½ teaspoon salt, and ¼ teaspoon pepper. Add ¼ cup water and the rosemary to the skillet. Lower the heat, cover, and cook for 30 to 45 minutes, until the potatoes are fork tender and fully cooked.

Divide the potatoes and rabbit legs among four plates and serve warm.

INGREDIENTS

6 tablespoons extra virgin olive oil, divided

½ cup diced carrots

½ cup diced celery

½ cup diced onion

4 rabbit legs

½ cup dry white wine

¾ cup chopped aromatic herbs, such as oregano, sage, rosemary, and marjoram

1 teaspoon salt, divided

½ teaspoon black pepper, divided

2 shallots, minced

1 clove garlic, minced

½ cup chopped bacon, about 3 slices

2 large russet potatoes, peeled and diced

¼ cup water

1 teaspoon minced rosemary

COSCIA DI FARAONA CON ASPARAGI
Leg of Guinea Fowl with Asparagus

You only have to look at this presentation to see this is a complete meal in itself: prosciutto, cheese, asparagus, and guinea fowl legs, with a rich sauce. You may also substitute chicken legs for this recipe if you can't find guinea fowl.

Serves 4

Preheat the oven to 350 degrees F.

Season the poultry with salt and pepper and set aside at room temperature.

Heat the olive oil in a large skillet over medium-high heat. Add the garlic, rosemary, and thyme, and stir about 2 to 3 minutes, until fragrant.

Place the poultry in a skillet over medium-high heat and brown well, about 3 to 5 minutes per side. Add enough white wine to cover the entire bottom of the skillet. Cover and reduce the heat to medium-low. Continue cooking 20 to 30 minutes, until a meat thermometer placed in the thickest part of the poultry leg reads 165 degrees F, and the meat is fork tender. Check during cooking and add a little hot water if needed.

While the poultry finishes cooking, fill a medium saucepan halfway with salted water, and bring to a boil over high heat. Snap the tough asparagus ends off where they naturally break and discard. Boil the remaining asparagus spears for 2 to 3 minutes then drain. They should not be cooked through at this point.

Spray a rimmed baking sheet with oil. Divide the asparagus into four bunches. Lay out slices of prosciutto on the baking sheet, and top with the grated cheese. Wrap a prosciutto slice around each asparagus bundle so the cheese is on the interior of the bundle. Bake for 5 to 7 minutes until the asparagus is tender, the ham is crispy, and the cheese is melted.

Serve the leg quarters along with the asparagus bundles and drizzle with sauce from the pan.

INGREDIENTS

4 guinea fowl leg quarters, or substitute 8 chicken drumsticks

½ teaspoon salt

¼ teaspoon black pepper

2 tablespoons extra virgin olive oil

1 clove garlic

2 sprigs fresh rosemary

2 sprigs fresh thyme

¼ to ½ cup white wine

1 bunch asparagus

4 slices prosciutto

½ cup grated Montasio or Parmigiano-Reggiano cheese

FRITTELLE DI MELE
Apple Fritters

I think of these sweet treats as Italian doughnuts! They can be served as dessert, and they're equally good with your morning espresso.

Serves 6 to 8

In a medium bowl, beat the egg with 1 tablespoon sugar. Add the milk, flour, cornstarch, baking powder, and the zest of half a lemon. Stir to fully combine and set the batter aside to rest for 1 hour.

Slice the apples horizontally leaving a hole in the center of each slice. Set slices aside and sprinkle with a few drops of lemon juice.

Heat the oil to 350 degrees F in a large skillet.

Using tongs, dip the apple slices into the batter, and fry them until golden, between 1 and 2 minutes on each side. Remove them to a paper towel-lined plate to drain and cool.

Arrange the apple fritters on a serving plate and sprinkle with powdered sugar. You may also garnish with whipped cream or your favorite custard.

INGREDIENTS

1 egg

1 tablespoon sugar

½ cup milk

¼ cup all-purpose flour, sifted

1 teaspoon cornstarch

2 teaspoons baking powder

Zest and juice of 1 lemon, halved

3 large Granny Smith apples, cored and peeled

2 cups peanut or vegetable oil

Powdered sugar, for sprinkling

Optional garnish: whipped cream or custard

A behind-the-scenes glimpse at the creation of the VIETRI Limoni collection.

CERAMICHE FABBRO

Created in 1919, the Ceramiche Fabbro company has been family-owned for five generations and continues to grow with the same enthusiasm and passion it has had from the start. Gianluca has experimented with historical styles throughout his tenure as maestro artisan, and his unique handsponging technique, now known distinctly as his own, captivates customers.

Gianluca's technique starts with medical-grade sponges cut and carved by hand (they are the perfect consistency for even application). Gianluca applies layers of paint to the sponge from light to dark with precise detail to evoke a sense of depth on each piece. Each sponge is used only once when paint is applied, allowing variation from one piece to the next—a beloved feature of VIETRI's handcrafted heritage. He carefully places the sponges piece by piece onto his chosen canvas, terra bianca, and then finishes with handpainted intricate details before the final piece is covered with a crystalline glaze and fired in the kiln for eight hours. The result is a true one-of-a-kind work of art for the table.

CHAPTER 9

Bringing Italy Home
SUSAN GRAVELY & BILL ROSS, NORTH CAROLINA

I SPEND MONTHS EACH YEAR TRAVELING THROUGHOUT
Italy, creating and imagining product designs, reveling in time with dear friends,
and enjoying incredible food. My time in Italy fills me up; I find the new creative
pursuits exhilarating, I sleep well, exercise well, and have a wonderful, life-giving
time. And yet, when it is time for me to leave and return
to the US, I do so happily. As my feet find North Carolina
soil, I know that I am home. Really home.

*I love trying to create a version
of Italy in our own Southern
home, with Italian paintings,
fragrances, pillows, clothing,
and—of course—with tableware.*

My time back in Chapel Hill gives me the
opportunity to absorb and embrace what I've noticed
and appreciated on my travels. I usually return with a
new treasure or two, as I love trying to create a version
of Italy in our own Southern home, with Italian paintings, fragrances, pillows,
clothing, and—of course—with tableware. More importantly, I return with fresh
enthusiasm to focus on my life's work of encouraging people to gather, to enjoy
meals around a table, and to celebrate life together. That is what Italy is about,
what VIETRI is about, what this book is about, and what I am about.

And so, when I come back home, I am eager to be with the people I have dearly
missed, to host in my own home, and to create some of that Italian magic around

*The living room in Susan and
Bill's home in Chapel Hill.
Opposite page: The table set for
a celebration with an heirloom
lace tablecloth purchased by
Susan's parents in Murano,
Italy in 1960.*

the table through hospitality and good food.

When Bill and I entertain, we delight in discussing the important aspects of a gathering, from the seating arrangement that will best encourage conversation to the courses that will best feature the season's bounty. Our menus at home always include some Italian dishes, along with a few of my Southern favorites.

Bill and I try to create a festive, fun, and relaxed atmosphere for our guests. Some of our most favorite parties have included complete strangers, but afterwards, they were strangers no more. To kick off the evening, we always begin with a prosecco toast. During the course of the meal, Bill usually asks our guests lots of questions that spark lively conversation. He likes to discover and delve into our friends' best vacations, favorite hikes, or childhood foibles. He is known for reading poems after dinner and encourages others to do the same. I am my happiest and truest self while at the table during these gatherings, talking and laughing with friends new and old.

VIETRI began when my mother and sister and I were mesmerized by those handpainted plates at the Il San Pietro Hotel in Positano. Those plates launched our business, and I have spent many, many work days dreaming up new designs for them, solving logistical issues for how to transport them, and selling them to top stores and customers around the world. Over the years, however, those plates have come to symbolize so much more for me. They are part of people's large holiday gatherings and intimate dinners for two. The plates are present for life's celebrations big and

small, and I feel that they represent connection, time together, and the savoring of life.

My life and my plate have been full of adventure, friendship, love, and learning. My hope for *Italy on a Plate* is that it will encourage you to try new recipes and enjoy them with friends and family. I hope my words have done Italy's wonders justice, and that they inspire you to travel there, soak in its splendor, and bring some of it back with you to share with those you love, around a table, with a full plate and a full heart.

Susan's kitchen looking out into the dining room and garden beyond.
Opposite page: Susan in her dinnerware pantry; Franco, the family's beloved Australian Labradoodle.

SCALLOPED OYSTERS

This casserole is a Southern classic. Unlike most casseroles, which rely on pantry staples like canned soup, rice, or pasta, this scalloped version uses fewer ingredients, highlighting the briny flavor of the fresh oysters. It can be prepared hours in advance, then covered and refrigerated. Just wait to add the last layer of breadcrumbs and the oyster liquid/cream mixture before popping it in the oven.

Serves 10 to 12

Preheat oven to 400 degrees F.

Combine the crushed saltines, dried onions, celery salt, black pepper, lemon juice, Worcestershire sauce, parsley, and melted butter in a medium bowl. Stir to fully mix and set aside.

Drain the oysters in a colander set over a bowl to capture the oyster liquor. Cut large oysters into two or three pieces. Set the oysters and liquor aside separately.

Butter an 8 x 8-inch baking dish. Cover the bottom with a layer of crumbs, top with a layer of oysters, then repeat the layering, ending with crumbs to top. Combine ½ cup of the oyster liquor with the half-and-half and pour over the casserole.

Bake for 30 to 35 minutes, until the casserole is bubbling and the breadcrumbs are lightly browned. Serve hot.

INGREDIENTS

1 sleeve saltines, crushed, about 2 cups

2 tablespoons minced dried onions

1 teaspoon celery salt

Dash of freshly ground black pepper

1 tablespoon lemon juice

1 tablespoon Worcestershire sauce

1 tablespoon chopped fresh Italian parsley

8 tablespoons (1 stick) unsalted butter, melted

1 quart oysters, liquor reserved

½ cup half-and-half

ROASTED LEG OF LAMB

The green olives are the best part of this recipe, one of my all-time favorites. If you are a huge olive lover like me, feel free to add extra olives. Make sure you start this recipe the day before you serve it in order to marinate the lamb properly.

Serves 8 to 10

Trim and discard excess fat from the lamb.

To make the marinade, combine the lime juice, garlic, ½ teaspoon salt, marjoram, and hot sauce in a small bowl.

Use a knife to gouge holes about ¾-inch deep on the sides and top of lamb. In each hole, pour some marinade and plug the hole with an olive.

In another small bowl, combine the remaining 1 teaspoon salt, seasoned salt, paprika, ginger, ground mustard, oregano, and pepper. Spread the rub over the top and sides of the leg of lamb. Cover the leg with plastic wrap and refrigerate overnight.

The next day, preheat the oven to 350 degrees F.

Transfer the lamb to a roasting pan and cook for 2 hours, or until a meat thermometer inserted in the meatiest part of the leg reads 145 degrees F.

Baste with marinade and hot water as needed.

Remove the meat from the pan and use the juices to make gravy, if desired. Slice and serve warm.

INGREDIENTS

1 (6-pound) leg of lamb

4 tablespoons lime juice

2 cloves garlic, minced

1½ teaspoons salt, divided

½ teaspoon marjoram

3 or 4 dashes hot sauce, your favorite brand

8 to 10 stuffed green olives

2 teaspoons Lawry's Seasoned Salt

1 tablespoon paprika

1 teaspoon ground ginger

½ teaspoon ground mustard

1 teaspoon oregano

1 teaspoon black pepper

SPINACH WITH ARTICHOKES

The smooth, nutty taste of a baked or boiled artichoke is one of my favorites. You can assemble this recipe early, and cover and refrigerate it for up to 8 hours; then remove, and let it come to room temperature an hour or so before baking.

Serves 8 to 10

Preheat the oven to 350 degrees F.

Cook the spinach according to package directions. Drain in a colander, and use paper towels to squeeze excess water out of the spinach. Set aside.

Mix the cream cheese and melted butter in the bowl of a mixer or food processor until smooth. Add the lemon juice, spinach, salt, pepper, seasoned salt, and nutmeg and mix to combine.

Place the artichoke hearts pointed ends up in a 11 x 7-inch baking dish. Spoon the spinach mixture over the top. Cover the baking dish with foil and pierce the foil with a few holes to vent.

Bake for 30 minutes. If desired, remove the foil and sprinkle cheese over the top, then continue baking about 5 minutes, until the cheese is melted.

INGREDIENTS

2 (10-ounce) packages chopped spinach

5 ounces (about ⅔ cup) cream cheese, at room temperature

3 tablespoons butter, melted

½ lemon, juiced

1 teaspoon Lawry's Seasoned Salt

½ teaspoon black pepper

1 teaspoon seasoned salt

Several dashes nutmeg

1 (14-ounce) can artichoke hearts, drained

Optional garnish: 1 cup shredded Parmigiano-Reggiano cheese

HOT MILK LAYER CAKE

This cake recipe and the following chocolate icing recipe belonged to my great-grandmother. I helped my mother make this cake for many holidays growing up in Rocky Mount, and it is still a favorite of guests and family.

Serves 8 to 10

Preheat oven to 320 degrees F.

Beat the eggs and sugar in a mixer 2 to 3 minutes until thick and creamy.

In a medium bowl, sift the flour, baking powder, and salt together. Gradually add this dry mixture to the egg mixture and mix until fully incorporated and the batter is smooth.

Heat the butter and milk in small saucepan over medium heat. Bring almost to the boiling point, then slowly add milk mixture to the cake batter in the mixing bowl (be careful not to splash!) and mix to combine. This will result in a very thin batter.

Spray two 8-inch cake pans with baking spray. Divide the batter between the two cake pans. Bake for 30 minutes, until a toothpick or skewer inserted in the center comes out clean.

Run a knife around the edges to easily remove the cakes from the pan and let the cakes cool on a wire rack.

Frost both layers of the cake with Grandmother's Chocolate Icing. Once the icing has set, serve.

INGREDIENTS

4 eggs

2 cups sugar

2 cups all-purpose flour

2 teaspoons baking powder

¼ teaspoon salt

½ cup (1 stick) unsalted butter

1 cup milk

Grandmother's Chocolate Icing (see recipe on page 226)

GRANDMOTHER'S CHOCOLATE ICING

Make sure to prepare this icing on a sunny day! If you make it on a rainy day, be aware that it may not set properly and may result in a thin consistency. Have a good candy thermometer on hand so that you achieve the soft-ball stage, and do not overcook.

Serves 8 to 10

Heat the butter, sugar, milk, and vanilla extract in a medium, heavy-bottomed saucepan over medium-low heat, stirring occasionally, about 10 to 13 minutes. Once the icing comes to a boil, cook without stirring for 1 minute.

Brush down the sides of the hot pan with a pastry brush dipped in warm water to remove sugar crystals. Turn off the heat. Stir in the chocolate until it is fully melted and incorporated.

Return the saucepan to medium-low heat and cook, without stirring, until the chocolate mixture reaches 234 degrees F, the soft-ball stage. This can take as long as 40 minutes, but do not stir. Use a candy thermometer so that you do not overcook.

While the chocolate mixture cooks, prepare an ice bath in a large bowl.

If you plan to beat the icing in the bowl of a standing mixer, pour the cooked chocolate mixture into that bowl. Otherwise, pour the chocolate into a large bowl and use a handheld mixer to beat until smooth. Place the bowl in the ice bath for 15 to 20 minutes.

Place the hot chocolate mixture in a separate bowl, and place the bowl in the ice bath to cool for 15 to 20 minutes until completely cooled.

Transfer the icing to the bowl of a standing mixer, and using the whisk attachment, beat on high speed for 3 to 5 minutes until it is a thick, pourable consistency. If it is too thick, add 1 to 2 tablespoons heavy cream and beat until you reach the desired consistency.

INGREDIENTS

8 tablespoons (1 stick) unsalted butter

3 cups sugar

1 ½ cups whole or 2 percent milk

1 teaspoon vanilla extract (optional)

3 ounces unsweetened baking chocolate

1 to 2 tablespoons heavy cream (as needed)

To ice the cake, spread ⅓ of the icing over the center of the bottom layer and use a spatula to push the icing to the edge. Add the second cake layer on top, and pour the remaining icing on top of that layer, allowing it to run down the sides. Smooth the icing with a spatula and fill in gaps as much as possible.

Let the icing cool to set before serving.

A portrait of Susan's mother, Lee, hangs above a portrait of Susan's great-grandmother in Susan and Bill's home.

GINGERBREAD COOKIES

My dear friend Merwyn's gingerbread recipe is pulled out every year. It is our tradition to make lots of shapes and flavors of cookies and then to invite families over to pick what they want from our laden table at home.

Yields 24

In a small bowl, whisk together the flour, baking powder, baking soda, salt, ginger, cinnamon, and cloves until well combined.

In the bowl of a stand mixer, or in a large bowl using a hand mixer, beat the butter, egg, and brown sugar on medium speed until well combined. Add the molasses, vanilla, and lemon zest and continue to blend on medium speed until smooth. Slowly stir in the dry ingredients from the small bowl, and beat on low until smooth.

Divide the dough in half and wrap each half in plastic. Let it rest at room temperature for 2 to 8 hours to meld the flavors. Note: the dough can be refrigerated for up to 4 days, then brought to room temperature before rolling out and baking.

When you are ready to bake, preheat the oven to 375 degrees F. Line a sheet pan (or 2 sheet pans if you are using both dough halves) with parchment.

Place one portion of the dough on a lightly floured surface. The dough will be sticky, so sprinkle it with a little flour. Also sprinkle your rolling pin with a little flour, and roll the dough out to a thickness of no more than ¼ inch. Sprinkle with additional flour if the dough is still sticky.

Use your choice of cookie cutters to cut your cookies and place them on the parchment-lined baking sheet about 2 inches apart.

Bake 7 to 10 minutes. Let them cool slightly in the pan until they are firm, then transfer the cookies to a rack to cool completely before decorating.

INGREDIENTS

3 cups all-purpose flour

1½ teaspoon baking powder

¾ teaspoon baking soda

¼ teaspoon salt

1½ tablespoons ground ginger

1¾ teaspoons cinnamon

¼ teaspoon ground cloves

6 tablespoons unsalted butter

1 large egg

¼ cup dark brown sugar

½ cup molasses

2 teaspoons vanilla

1 teaspoon finely grated lemon zest

ALESSANDRO'S WORKSHOP

Sometimes you meet someone who is an immediate kindred spirit. Alessandro Taddei is one of those people. A dear friend with a twinkling energy, Alessandro is the originator of Old St. Nick, VIETRI's beloved holiday dinnerware collection. It all started one afternoon in his workshop when I came to him with my idea for a gentle and genuine, active and authentic Santa, one who chopped down wood and planted trees, one who made toys for children and woodland creatures, and one who was as true to his friends as they were to him. I dreamed of a Santa who cooked delicious meals, explored the world, and thought deeply about how to make it a better place. Alessandro understood this vision.

After a few months, I returned to Alessandro's workshop to see what he had come up with for Old St. Nick. Alessandro had taken my idea and turned it into something even better. I was completely charmed by the designs, and I am thrilled that the collection has become a cherished part of so many families' holiday traditions.

Ten years after the Old St. Nick ceramics collection launched, Alessandro and I wanted to do something new together. Some of my dearest childhood memories are of reading books with my parents, so we began to talk about a series of Old St. Nick children's books. Bill and I would have wonderful pasta lunches together with Alessandro's lovely wife, Franca, dreaming up plotlines, characters, adventures, and rhymes.

Since the initial idea, we have created five books together. Typically, I work on the story's words and then send a rough draft to Alessandro. I take no offense when he reduces the word count by about half (!) because he manages to capture the message and suffuse it with great Italian spirit through his fabulous illustrations. We both love that the books share life lessons—reminders to be kind, to value our families, to be stewards of the earth, and to love one another.

Clockwise from top: Alessandro adds the finishing touches on an illustration for an Old St. Nick children's book; Susan with Alessandro and his daughter, Sara, and wife, Franca; Alessandro handpaints an Old St. Nick piece during a VIETRI Artisan Event.

INDEX

Page numbers in italics indicate photographs.
Please refer to page 238 for an index of VIETRI collections featured in this book.

INDEX OF VIETRI COLLECTIONS

Italy on a Plate features beloved collections from **VIETRI**'s earliest days to today. For more information on the collections and what is currently available, please visit **VIETRI**.com.

THE WORK OF MANY HANDS

ITALY ON A PLATE—AND THAT PLATE HAS BEEN MY JOURNEY!
In the early days of VIETRI, Frances and I knew we wanted counsel from those seasoned in business. We made a list of our father's friends who had family businesses and who had demonstrated resilience, dedication, and acumen, and we asked them to be on our Board of Directors. I am indebted to and deeply thankful for Chris Harris, Uncle Bob Allen, Jack Bailey, Garry Snook, Ray Jones, and RB Fitch. Immense thanks to our current Board—Lisa Church, Jerry Bell, Joyce Fitzpatrick, Bill Moore, and Jeff Little. And gratitude to my cousin, Elizabeth Troutman, whom I have admired for her brilliance and spirit for all her life.

To the dear friends who have advised me, championed me, and understood my passion and crazy work life, thank you. You have traveled with me, purchased VIETRI from the beginning, and kept my spirits up during challenging times. My heartfelt thanks goes to Frances Mayes—marvelous, meaningful, mesmerizing Mrs. Mayes. Sharlie and Todd Robbins, thank you for accompanying me to that very first meeting with Bloomingdale's. Marree and John Townsend, thank you for explaining an asset and liability to me on a park bench in New York and being the first to purchase Campagna. Katie and Walker Morris, thank you for your early business tips. To Moyra and Brian Kileff, you have always believed in my actions and trade. To Tim and Sara Belk, Kitty Bell, Claudia Little, and Beth Dowdle, thank you for your relentless encouragement. To Nettie Burnette, our "house heart," and to Merwyn Varnado, thank you for keeping our home running, our family organized, and our spirits up.

None of this would be possible without my VIETRI family. Far more than employees, I consider each one of you a friend. Thank you to Lisa Boyles, who took this project on with voracity and excitement. Great gratitude to Janice Shay and to Brette Baumhover for carrying this project on your shoulders. Thank you, Heather Hutchins, for matching my voice, and Mollie Baker for your incredible design eye. To Holli Draughn and Natalie Riddick, thank you for being yourselves with push and enthusiasm. Our Italian team, thank you for your creativity—Sara Guarracino, Chiara Battistini, Giulia Montali, Annette Joseph, and Barbara Pederzini. And to our American team—thanks to Andrea Weigl, Lynn Wells, Merwyn Varnado, Susan Johnson Smith, Robin Welch, and Felicia Trujillo. Thank you all for making this dream a reality. A special thank you to Lisa and Sally Ekus and Carrie Bachman for directing us to make this book as special as it is.

And to my beloved Italians: there are so many beyond those in this book whom I consider family. I have been in your homes. I have been on vacations with you. I have laughed and cried with you! *Grazie per tutti voi. Grazie di cuore!*

To my stepdaughters, Amanda and Rebecca Ross, thank you for welcoming me into your lives. To my "baby" brother, Page Gravely, thank you for your teasing and charismatic style. To my sisters and brothers-in-law, Donna Gravely, Betsy and Steve Frazier, Libby and Willard Ross: Travels with you are some of my fondest memories. To my nieces and nephews, Lee and Helen Frankstone, Susan and Shaw Hargett, Roman Gravely, Hannah and Jeff Clarke, and Ferebee and Will Plyler, thank you for bringing such fun to my life with your youth, beautiful children, and enthusiasm for Italy.

To Frances, my dear sister, loyal business partner, and true friend, none of this would have been possible without your daring sense of adventure and zest for living life well. We have been with each other through thick and thin, and I am so lucky to be on this amazing ride with you.

To my father, Daddy: You taught me to be curious about the world and gave me the confidence to pursue my wildest dreams by always making me feel safe and secure. To Momma, my greatest cheerleader, truest inspiration, and closest friend: I miss you every moment of every day.

And finally, and especially, to Bill Ross, my dear husband. You love me unconditionally, as I love you. From inspiring me with poetry to prose, from traveling with me from one Italian town to another, from understanding when work has to come first to encouraging me to pause and take a rest, I am so glad to share this life with you.

As we always say at VIETRI, this is truly the work of many hands, and I am so grateful. The world is now a complete circle for me.